The Growth and Influence of Islam

IN THE NATIONS OF ASIA AND CENTRAL ASIA

Indonesia

The Growth and Influence of Islam

IN THE NATIONS OF ASIA AND CENTRAL ASIA

Afghanistan

Azerbaijan

Bangladesh

Indonesia

Islam in Asia: Facts and Figures

Islamism and Terrorist Groups in Asia

Kazakhstan

The Kurds

Kyrgyzstan

Malaysia

Muslims in China

Muslims in India

Muslims in Russia

Pakistan

Tajikistan

Turkmenistan

Uzbekistan

The Growth and Influence of Islam
IN THE NATIONS OF ASIA AND CENTRAL ASIA

Indonesia

Lynda Cohen Cassanos

Mason Crest Publishers
Philadelphia

Produced by OTTN Publishing, Stockton, New Jersey

Mason Crest Publishers
370 Reed Road
Broomall, PA 19008
www.masoncrest.com

First printing

1 3 5 7 9 8 6 4 2

Library of Congress Cataloging-in-Publication Data

Cassanos, Lynda Cohen.
  Indonesia / Lynda Cohen Cassanos.
      p. cm. — (The growth and influence of Islam in the nations of Asia and Central
Asia)
  Includes bibliographical references and index.
  ISBN 1-59084-835-7
  1. Indonesia—Juvenile literature. I. Title. II. Series.
  DS615.C37 2005
  959.8—dc22
                                    2004019848

Table of Contents

An Indonesian soldier walks through rubble at the site of a terrorist bombing on the island of Bali. The October 2002 blast outside a busy nightclub in a tourist area killed more than 202 people and injured hundreds of others. As a predominantly Muslim nation that is secular and moderate, Indonesia has become an important battleground in the war on terrorism.

Dr. Harvey Sicherman, president and director of the Foreign Policy Research Institute, is the author of such books as *America the Vulnerable: Our Military Problems and How to Fix Them* (2002) and *Palestinian Autonomy, Self-Government and Peace* (1993).

Introduction

by Dr. Harvey Sicherman

America's triumph in the Cold War promised a new burst of peace and prosperity. Indeed, the decade between the demise of the Soviet Union and the destruction of September 11, 2001, proved deceptively hopeful. Today, of course, we are more fully aware—to our sorrow—of the dangers and troubles no longer just below the surface.

The Muslim identities of most of the terrorists at war with the United States have also provoked great interest in Islam as well as the role of religion in politics. It is crucial for Americans not to assume that Osama bin Laden's ideas are identical to those of most Muslims or, for that matter, that most Muslims are Arabs. A truly world religion, Islam claims hundreds of millions of adherents, from every ethnic group scattered across the globe. This book series covers the growth and influence of Muslims in Asia and Central Asia.

A glance at the map establishes the extraordinary coverage of our authors. Every climate and terrain may be found, along with every form of human society, from the nomadic groups of the Central Asian steppes to

highly sophisticated cities such as Singapore, New Delhi, and Shanghai. The economies of the nations examined in this series are likewise highly diverse. In some, barter systems are still used; others incorporate modern stock markets. In some of the countries, large oil reserves hold out the prospect of prosperity. Other countries, such as India and China, have progressed by moving from a government-controlled to a more market-based economic system. Still other countries have built wealth on service and shipping.

Central Asia and Asia is a heavily armed and turbulent area. Three of its states (China, India, and Pakistan) are nuclear powers, and one (Kazakhstan) only recently rid itself of nuclear weapons. But it is also a place where the horse and mule remain indispensable instruments of war. All of the region's states have an extensive history of conflict, domestic and international, old and new. Afghanistan, for example, has known little but invasion and civil war over the past two decades.

Governments include dictatorships, democracies, and hybrids without a name; centralized and decentralized administrations; and older patterns of tribal and clan associations. The region is a veritable encyclopedia of political expression.

Although such variety defies easy generalities, it is still possible to make several observations. First, the geopolitics of Central Asia and Asia reflect the impact of empires and the struggles of post-imperial independence. Central Asia, a historic corridor for traders and soldiers, was the scene of Russian expansion well into Soviet times. While Kazakhstan's leaders participated in the historic meeting of December 25, 1991, that dissolved the Soviet Union, the rest of the region's newly independent republics hardly expected it. They have found it difficult to grapple with a sometimes tenuous independence, buffeted by a strong residual Russian influence, the absence of settled institutions, the temptation of newly valuable natural resources, and mixed populations lacking a solid national identity. The shards of the Soviet Union have often been sharp—witness the Russian war in Chechnya—and sometimes fatal for those ambitious to grasp them.

Moving further east, one encounters an older devolution, that of the half-century since the British Raj dissolved into India and Pakistan (the latter giving violent birth to Bangladesh in 1971). Only recently, partly under the impact of the war on terrorism, have these nuclear-armed neighbors and adversaries found it possible to renew attempts at reconciliation. Still further east, Malaysia shares a British experience, but Indonesia has been influenced by its Dutch heritage. Even China defines its own borders along the lines of the Qing empire (the last pre-republican dynasty) at its most expansionist (including Tibet and Taiwan). These imperial histories lie heavily upon the politics of the region.

A second aspect worth noting is the variety of economic experimentation afoot in the area. State-dominated economic strategies, still in the ascendant, are separating government from the actual running of commerce and industry. "Privatization," however, is frequently a byword for crony capitalism and corruption. Yet in dynamic economies such as that of China, as well as an increasingly productive India, hundreds of millions of people have dramatically improved both their standard of living and their hope for the future. All of them aspire to benefit from international trade. Competitive advantages, such as low-cost labor (in some cases trained in high technology) and valuable natural resources (oil, gas, and minerals), promise much. This is indeed a revolution of rising expectations, some of which are being satisfied.

Yet more than corruption threatens this progress. Population increase, even though moderating, still overwhelms educational and employment opportunities. Many countries are marked by extremes of wealth and poverty, especially between rural and urban areas. Dangerous jealousies threaten ethnic groups (such as anti-Chinese violence in Indonesia).

Hopelessly overburdened public services portend turmoil. Public health, never adequate, is harmed further by environmental damage to critical resources (such as the Aral Sea). By and large, Central Asian and Asian countries are living well beyond their infrastructures.

Third and finally, Islam has deeply affected the states and peoples of the region. Indonesia is the largest Muslim state in the world, and India hosts the second-largest Muslim population. Islam is not only the official religion of many states, it is the very reason for Pakistan's existence. But Islamic practices and groups vary: the well-known Sunni and Shiite groups are joined by energetic Salafi (Wahabi) and Sufi movements. Over the last 20 years especially, South and Central Asia have become battle-grounds for competing Shiite (Iranian) and Wahabi (Saudi) doctrines, well financed from abroad and aggressively antagonistic toward non-Muslims and each other. Resistance to the Soviet invasion of Afghanistan brought these groups battle-tested warriors and organizers. The war on terrorism has exposed just how far-reaching and active the new advocates of holy war (jihad) can be. Indonesia, in particular, is the scene of rivalry between an older, tolerant Islam and the jihadists. But Pakistan also faces an Islamic identity crisis. And India, wracked by sectarian strife, must hold together its democratic framework despite Muslim and Hindu extremists. This newly significant struggle within Islam, superimposed on an older Muslim history, will shape political and economic destinies throughout the region and beyond. Hence, the focus of our series.

We hope that these books will enlighten both teacher and student about a critical subject in a critical area of the world. Central Asia and Asia would be important in their own right to Americans; arguably, after 9/11, they became vital to our national security. And the enduring impact of Islam is a crucial factor we must understand. We at the Foreign Policy Research Institute hope these books will illuminate both the facts and the prospects.

Light filters through stained-glass windows to reveal the elegant Moroccan-style interior of Masjid Raya, the largest mosque in Sumatra. Indonesia is home to more than 200 million Muslims, the world's largest Muslim population.

1

Place in the World

If you were asked, "What country has the largest Muslim population?" would you know the answer? If you learned the same nation is home to the world's largest **archipelago**, the world's most volcanic region, the world's longest lizard, and the world's largest flower, would these clues help? If you did not know the answer was Indonesia, you are not alone. Most people know very little about this vast island nation, though it is the largest country in Southeast Asia and the world's fourth most populous nation.

The name *Indonesia* is formed from two Greek words: *Indos*, which means "India," and *nesos*, which means "islands." The Republic of Indonesia is a string of over 17,000 islands that form a crescent-like shape across the equator. The islands are situated one-third above the equator and two-thirds below, between the Indian Ocean and the Pacific Ocean. Indonesia shares three islands with other countries: one-third of Borneo, where Indonesia's Kalimantan province is located, belongs to Malaysia; Irian Jaya (also called Papua) is the western half of Papua New Guinea; and independent East Timor is adjacent to West Timor. Indonesia is strategically located in the southern waters between India and China, two countries that have had a profound impact on the the archipelago's economy, religion, and culture throughout history.

The country's motto, *Bhinneka Tunggal Ika* ("unity in diversity"), signifies the challenge faced by a nation that includes dozens of major ethnic groups and hundreds of minor ones. The motto stresses the solidarity of the Indonesian people despite their many cultural and ethnic differences. Although a few regions have active separatist movements, there is generally a strong sense of national unity. The country's coat of arms features a *garuda,* a mythical golden eagle from ancient Hindu epics, clutching a banner with the national motto in its talons. The 17 feathers on each wing, 8 feathers on the tail, and 45 on the neck represent the date of Indonesia's proclamation of independence: August 17, 1945.

Large Muslim populations can be found in other Asian countries, such as Pakistan, Bangladesh, and India, but more than 230 million Muslims—over 20 percent of the world's Islamic population—live in Southeast Asia. Of these, more than 200 million Muslims live in Indonesia.

Islam is a relatively young religion in Indonesia, compared to its history in many countries in Asia and the Middle East. Islam did not take hold in the archipelago until the 13th century, when it was introduced by traders. (In many other areas the religion spread through military conquest.) Even then, its observance was for the most part fused with the practices of established religions like Hinduism and Buddhism, as well as with **indigenous** beliefs such as **animism**. Islam has become an important

An Indonesian man reads a newspaper filled with reports about the country's first direct presidential election, held in July 2004. In September of that year, former army general Susilo Bambang Yudhoyono won a runoff election with 61 percent of the vote, defeating incumbent president Megawati Sukarnoputri.

source of identity in Indonesia, yet it is often practiced in a less rigid manner than the way it is observed in some other Muslim nations.

Like the United States, Indonesia may be called a *secular* state. More exactly, it is a multi-religious state, where only atheism is impermissible. The population is 88 percent Muslim and there are numerous Islamic political parties, but the majority of the voting public favors a nonreligious government and does not want the laws of Islam to dictate civil life.

Indonesia is a land of extremes and contradictions with an intricate history and rich culture. There is widespread poverty and the country is burdened by a struggling economy, political corruption, and separatist violence. The country's health care and educational systems are in need of repair. And although Indonesia has a moderate Muslim majority, radical Islamic and terrorist groups are active in the archipelago.

However, Indonesia has a wealth of spectacular scenery and wildlife, as well as great natural resources such as oil, gas, tin, rubber, copper, and gold. It is also strategically located along one of the world's most valuable shipping routes. The nation's strong workforce and increasingly educated population support an emerging democracy. In 2004, Indonesia had its first direct presidential elections. The freedom, fairness, and massive turnout of the elections were widely considered a major step toward democracy.

Sprouted rice has just been transplanted into these flooded paddys in western Java; a crop at a later stage is visible in the background to the right. The warm climate and fertile soil of the Indonesian islands make them ideal for cultivation of rice and other crops.

2

The Land

Viewed from above, Indonesia resembles a necklace of unique emerald-colored jewels strung between the Indian Ocean on the south and west and the Pacific Ocean on the north and east. This island nation spans the waters from the continents of Asia to Australia and straddles the equator for one-eighth of the earth's circumference.

Indonesia extends over an area wider than the United States. The country stretches east to west approximately 3,175 miles (5,120 km) and north to south about 1,090 miles (1,760 km). The islands themselves cover a land area of approximately 705,006 square miles (1,826,440 sq km) and the waters span about 35,898 square miles (93,000 sq km). Indonesia is one of the few countries in the world to contain such great expanses of water—the country's indigenous name, *Tanah Air Kita,* means "our earth and water."

Indonesia stretches across three time zones. Because it lies on the equator, there is little change in the length of day from one season to the next, and there is only a 48-minute difference between the longest and the shortest days of the year. (By comparison, there is a six-hour difference between those days in New York.)

This expansive archipelago consists of over 17,000 islands, of which about 6,000 are inhabited. They vary in size from tiny islets and atolls to islands that are larger than Spain. Indonesia's five main islands are Sumatra, Irian Jaya, Sulawesi (formerly called Celebes), Kalimantan, and Java. These islands encompass approximately 92 percent of the nation's land area and support about 94 percent of the population. Irian Jaya, the Indonesian province on the eastern island of Papua New Guinea, is part of the world's second-largest island, after Greenland. Kalimantan is the southern two-thirds of Borneo, which is the world's third-largest island.

Geologists believe that hundreds of millions of years ago the earth consisted of one landmass. In time it divided into two huge continents. One included what would become Africa, South America, Australia, and Antarctica; the other would become Asia, Europe, and North America. About 15 million years ago, shifts and collisions of land under the ocean and volcanic eruptions resulted in the further separation of these super-continents into smaller landmasses. These included the islands of what is called today Indonesia.

The islands are grouped into three areas. The Sunda Shelf is an extension of the Malay Peninsula and the Southeast Asian mainland, which contains Sumatra, Java, Madura, and Kalimantan. The Sahul Shelf is the northwestern extension of the Australian landmass, where Irian Jaya is located. The third area lies between the two shelves, home to Sulawesi, the Nusa Tenggara archipelago, and Maluku (formerly called the Moluccas).

Each region of Indonesia abounds in spectacular scenery. Sumatra offers breathtaking mountains and many rivers and lakes. A chain of volcanoes

This aerial view shows several of the smaller Indonesian islands, including Lomblen (top), Adonara (center), Solor (right), and Flores (bottom).

that begins on the west coast of Sumatra slices through the interior of neighboring Java, providing a dramatic background to the island's fertile green fields and rice terraces. Magnificent plants grow on Kalimantan, which also has forbidding wetlands and mangrove forests. Sulawesi is home to the towering mountains of Tana Toraja, and, off the Nusa Tenggara's Lombok Islands, the Gili Islands have exquisite coral reefs that attract snorkelers and divers.

Lush and fertile Bali differs from the drier climate and terrain of the other islands of Nusa Tenggara. The hundreds of small islands of Maluku, sometimes referred to as the Spice Islands, have the distinction of being the only place where cloves, mace, and nutmeg were originally grown. And the rich coral and marine life in the sea around Irian Jaya provides a striking

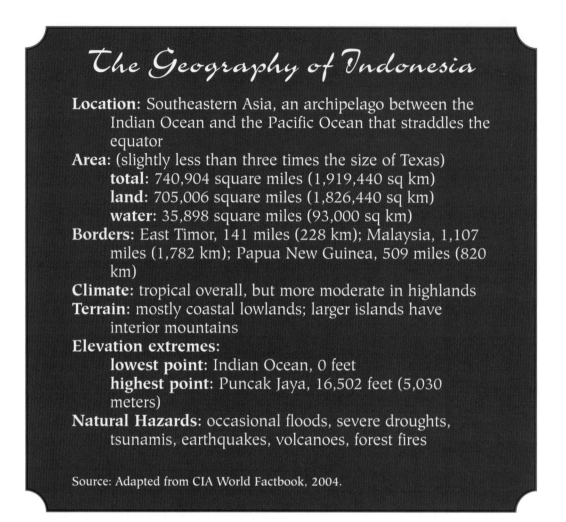

The Geography of Indonesia

Location: Southeastern Asia, an archipelago between the Indian Ocean and the Pacific Ocean that straddles the equator

Area: (slightly less than three times the size of Texas)
  total: 740,904 square miles (1,919,440 sq km)
  land: 705,006 square miles (1,826,440 sq km)
  water: 35,898 square miles (93,000 sq km)

Borders: East Timor, 141 miles (228 km); Malaysia, 1,107 miles (1,782 km); Papua New Guinea, 509 miles (820 km)

Climate: tropical overall, but more moderate in highlands

Terrain: mostly coastal lowlands; larger islands have interior mountains

Elevation extremes:
  lowest point: Indian Ocean, 0 feet
  highest point: Puncak Jaya, 16,502 feet (5,030 meters)

Natural Hazards: occasional floods, severe droughts, tsunamis, earthquakes, volcanoes, forest fires

Source: Adapted from CIA World Factbook, 2004.

contrast to its inhospitable jungle terrain of the interior.

There are all kinds of geographical features found throughout the archipelago: tropical rainforests, volcanoes, coastal lowlands, wetlands, jungles, coral reefs, mangrove swamps, high plains, and beaches. In Irian Jaya, there are even year-round snow-capped mountains. Nearly the entire archipelago is mountainous, with volcanoes defining the horizon. The highest peak in Southeast Asia is Irian Jaya's Puncak Jaya, which reaches some 16,502 feet (5,030 meters) high. Impressive mountains are also located in Central Sulawesi and north-central Kalimantan.

Volcanoes

It is said that most Indonesians live and die within sight of a volcano. As part of the most volcanic region of the world, Indonesia has about 130 active volcanoes (another 270 are extinct, or non-active). The archipelago extends through a part of the western Pacific known as the "Ring of Fire," a chain of volcanoes that encircle the Pacific Basin. The volcanoes form a crescent-shaped line that travels the length of Sumatra and Java, down to Bali, through Nusa Tenggara, then northward into Maluku, Sulawesi, and finally the Philippines. Java has the most active volcanoes; those east of it are less active, although Nusa Tengarra and North Sulawesi have numerous active volcanoes. As a result of this volcanic activity, Indonesia also experiences earthquakes and the occasional tsunami, or huge tidal wave.

Indonesia's most famous volcano, Krakatau (also spelled *Krakatoa*), erupted in 1883 with the loudest bang ever recorded on earth and a force equal to several hydrogen bombs. Krakatau is located in the Sunda Strait between Java and Sumatra, and its eruption was heard in Australia, over 2,000 miles (3,220 km) away. Volcanic ash fell as far as Singapore, about 520 miles (840 km) to the north. Over 36,000 people were killed, massive tidal waves destroyed parts of the coasts of Java and Sumatra, and ash clouds swept around the globe for over a year.

In 1815 Gunung Tambora, a volcano on the north coast of Sumbawa in Nusa Tenggara, erupted. It released an immense amount of ash and **pumice**, and over 92,000 people died on Sumbawa and the neighboring island of Lombok as a result of ensuing diseases and famine. The ash clouds lowered global temperatures, causing a "year without summer" in the United States and other parts of the world.

After being dormant for over 140 years, Gunung Agung in Bali erupted in 1963, killing about 1,500 people and spreading lava and cinders over half of the island. Some islanders saw the destruction as a sign of the wrath of God. To this day, in East Java the Tenggerese people offer a sacrifice to appease the smoking volcanic crater.

Although the volcanoes wreak much destruction, they also contribute to the ecology of Indonesia. Perhaps the greatest gifts of the menacing volcanoes are their nutrient-rich ash and lava. In many places, they help replace the minerals in the soil that are washed downstream throughout the year. As a result, the soil in Indonesia is among the most fertile in the world. However, if the chemical composition of the volcanic discharge is acidic, as it is in Central and South Sumatra, it is not beneficial.

An island's agricultural productivity and the size of its population bear a direct correlation to the number of nearby volcanoes and the quality of their lava. For example, Java has the most active volcanoes and the richest soil. It also has the highest rice yields and population. Using the **sawah** method of wet rice cultivation, farmers on Java and Bali harvest two to three rice crops a year. There is a saying among native Indonesians that if one shoves a stick in the ground on these fertile islands, it will produce leaves.

Extinct volcanoes often have spectacularly colored lakes in their craters caused by the mix of minerals and water. The Kelimutu volcano on the island of Flores in Nusa Tenggara has three crater lakes near its summit at 5,246 feet (1,600 meters). The lakes are known to change colors, and at various times have been red, blue, and green; turquoise, green, and black; and blue, red-brown, and light brown. The cooled lava rock on Java is good for carving, which facilitated the construction of Hindu monuments over the course of several centuries.

Rainforests, Lakes, and Rivers

The hot and humid climate, fertile soil, and predictable rainfall have enabled the growth of many large rainforests in Indonesia. The country is second only to Brazil in total area of rainforests. Almost two-thirds of

The mouth of this extinct volcano has filled with water, becoming a brightly colored crater lake. Indonesia is home to hundreds of volcanoes and is part of the Pacific "Ring of Fire."

Indonesia is covered by swamp, woodland, and tropical rainforest, most of which lies in Sumatra, Kalimantan, Sulawesi, and Irian Jaya. The tallest trees in the rainforests grow over 150 feet (46 meters) tall. Over the centuries, large sections of the rainforests on Java and Bali have been cleared for rice fields. Today, the country's remaining tropical forests are endangered due to local and foreign timber companies, mining, population relocation, and agriculture. A 2002 environmental report concluded that Indonesia is losing almost 4.9 million acres (roughly 2 million hectares) of forest every year—an area equal to half the size of Switzerland.

In addition to rainforests, Sumatra contains a series of volcanic lakes, including the massive Lake Toba. The largest lake in Southeast Asia, covering 502 square miles (1,300 sq km), Lake Toba is nestled in a valley between two parallel chains of the high Bukit Barisan mountain range. In Sulawesi, Lake Matano has the richest iron deposits in Southeast Asia. Rivers such as the Digul in Irian Jaya provide primary transportation routes in heavily forested areas and are important sources of irrigation in this mostly agricultural land.

Climate

Because Indonesia lies on the equator, it has a tropical climate that is usually hot and humid throughout the year. The temperature in any one location rarely changes more than a few degrees. Indonesia's weather is characterized by two seasons: the dry season and the rainy season. The dry season lasts from about May to October and is influenced by the Australian air masses—large bodies of air that maintain uniform properties of moisture and temperature. The wet season lasts from around December to March and is shaped by mainland Asian and Pacific Ocean air masses. During this season it may rain in sudden tropical downpours and then be dry for the rest of the day, or it may rain for days. The heaviest rainfall usually occurs in December and January. The weather between seasons is a transitional mix of sun-filled days and thunderstorms.

The amount of rainfall a region receives is based on the intensity of the monsoons—the winds that bring the heavy rains of the wet season. The western and northern parts of the country generally have the most rainfall due to the moisture-packed monsoon clouds that travel through the region. Western Sumatra, Java, Bali, and the interiors of Kalimantan and Sulawesi may receive more than 80 inches (200 centimeters) of rain annually. Bogor, a city near Jakarta on Java, has the world's highest number of rainstorms—on average 322 a year. The islands closest to Australia and Nusa Tenggara are the driest regions, with less than 40 inches (100 cm) of rain per year. The islands of southern Maluku experience an unpredictable rainfall. Timor Island, home of the provincial capital of Nusa Tenggara Barat, Kupang, is particularly susceptible to typhoons.

In certain areas—far south of the equator and in the highlands—Indonesia has what some consider a cold season during the months of July and August. Throughout the rest of the country, year-round temperatures at sea level range from about 70° to 90° Fahrenheit (20° to 32°

Celsius) and humidity averages 75 to 85 percent. The temperatures in the hills are on average six to twelve degrees cooler, and the highest mountain ranges are always snow-capped.

Plant Life

Indonesia is located in a large botanical region known as Melanesia, an area that also includes the Philippines, all of Papua New Guinea except the Solomon Islands, and parts of the Malay Peninsula. The flora of Indonesia differs from other tropical regions of the world, as well as from that of Asia and Australia. There are about 40,000 species of plants in Indonesia, with 5,000 species on Java alone. About 6,000 species are used by Indonesians as raw materials for herbal medicines, handicrafts, and items in traditional ceremonies.

The largest flower in the world, the rafflesia, thrives in the forests of Sumatra. This parasitic plant can grow up to three feet (almost one meter) across and weigh up to 20 pounds (9 kilograms). Swedish explorer Eric Mjoberg described this flower as having "a penetrating smell more repulsive than any buffalo carcass in an advanced state of decomposition." A similar plant to the rafflesia, the corpse plant, exudes a scent that smells like a dead animal to attract insects. Other plants include many species of insect-trapping pitcher plants. In the humid rainforest environment, hibiscus, jasmine, allemande, bougainvillea, frangipani, and lotus lilies grow profusely in the fertile soil. The country's thousands of species of orchids include the largest kind, the tiger orchid, as well as the tiny, leafless species known as *Taeniophyllum*. In addition, the fertile forest floor breeds a vast array of fungi, including the horsehair blight, sooty mold, and black mildew.

Indonesia is an important source of timber and home to approximately 30,000 species of trees such as sandalwood, ebony, teakwood, and **rattan**. Some trees have a cultural as well as an ecological significance. For example, the Banyan tree, an unusual-looking tree with long gnarled roots that grow from its branches to the ground, is associated with authority and thought by some to be inhabited by spirits.

Indonesia's green landscape is perhaps its greatest resource. Owing to the effects of strong sunlight, constant humidity, and fertile volcanic soil, growth is constant and rapid throughout the islands. According to travel writer Bill Dalton, "When you build a fence in Indonesia six months later it is not a fence. It is a living wall of vegetation."

Animal Life

Millions of years ago, sea-level changes, coastal erosion, shifts in land, and volcanoes caused animals of Asia and Australia to migrate through the Indonesian islands. Various species traveled to the islands and then were trapped by changing tides. Eventually, some even developed their own characteristics after eons of isolation. As a result, Indonesia is one of the most diverse and celebrated animal habitats in the world. It is home to over 500 species of mammals, 3,000 species of fish, and 1,500 species of birds. Orangutans, rhinoceroses, giant sea turtles, mammoth butterflies, and flesh-eating lizards are just a few examples of the exotic wildlife that can be found on the islands.

In the mid-1800s European naturalists began to study Indonesia's *flora* and *fauna*. Alfred Russel Wallace, a noted British naturalist, visited the islands between 1854 and 1862. He was the first to classify the Indonesian archipelago

The Komodo dragon is native to a few of Indonesia's islands. This carnivorous predator is the world's largest lizard, as males grow to an average of about eight feet and 300 pounds.

into two ecological zones: the Eastern Australian Zone and the Western Asian Zone. The hypothetical Wallace Line established the Makassar Strait and the Lombok Strait as the line separating the animals originally from Asia and those originally from Australia. Of the Lombok Strait, Wallace wrote in 1858, "The strait is here fifteen miles wide, so that we may pass in two hours from one great division of earth to another, differing as essentially in their animal life as Europe does from America."

West of the Wallace Line, the animals on the lush islands of Sumatra, Java, Kalimantan, and Bali resemble those of Asia. Large mammals such as Asian elephants, tigers, tapirs, one- and two-horned rhinoceros, proboscis monkeys with long noses, and orangutans with bright orange shaggy coats inhabit the area. The Balinese have a saying about the eastern end of their small island, "Here the tigers end."

East of the Wallace Line, the more arid regions of Lombok and Irian Jaya are inhabited by cockatoos, birds of paradise, crocodiles, frilled lizards, and tree kangaroos that can dash up trees and jump from one tree to the next. The Komodo dragon, the world's longest lizard, is found on the southeastern islands of Flores, Gili, Motang, Komodo, and Rinca. This giant monitor lizard can grow to a length of 6 to 10 feet (2 to 3 meters) and briefly run just over 11 miles (18 km) an hour—as fast, or faster, than a human. The babirusa, a tusked boar; and the anoa, a dwarf buffalo, are found on the island of Sulawesi, which lies in a transitional zone. Mountain goats, wild warthogs, sun bears, and miniature deer only 14 inches (35 cm) are among the other mammals that inhabit the archipelago.

The Indonesian government is making an effort to protect much of its endangered wildlife. The country has 33 national parks and nature, marine, and wildlife reserves. There are several orangutan rehabilitation centers, such as Camp Leakey in Tanjung Putting, Kalimantan's national park, and North Sumatra's Gunung Leuser, a park that also provides a home for endangered Sumatran rhinos, tigers, and elephants.

Indonesian islands were once centers of both Hindu and Buddhist kingdoms. In Central Java, the Sailendra dynasty built a Buddhist monument they called Borobudhur during the eighth and ninth centuries.

3

The History

In 1891, on the island of Java, a Dutch scientist named Eugene Dubois discovered fossils that resembled human bones. The remains of "Java Man," named after the island on which they found, were evidence of a species called *Homo erectus* that existed in the region as early as 1.8 million years ago.

The first modern humans to inhabit the archipelago were probably ancestors of the current inhabitants of the Irian Jayan highlands. Anthropologists have theorized that they may have come from the Asian mainland 40,000 years ago.

The first recorded southward migration of people from Asia began about 4,000 years ago. These seafaring people, speaking various closely related languages, settled most of the archipelago, as well as the Malay Peninsula and the Philippines. The settlers introduced refined stone tools to the indigenous population. By about 500 B.C. immigrants from China brought bronze, then iron, to the islands. Eventually small village governments were organized. These were often based around the community's system of wet rice cultivation. Some of the migrants traveled into the remote, mountainous interiors where they practiced a nomadic, slash-and-burn type of agriculture.

The islands' coastal inhabitants, called Orang Laut (Indonesian for "people of the sea"), are thought to have sailed to other regions as early as the seventh century B.C. Destinations included those as far away as India, Madagascar, and Polynesia. These seafarers established trade routes between the islands of the archipelago and along inland tributaries. The impact of the sea trade on Indonesia remained strong for several centuries.

Hinduism and Buddhism

Early Indonesians were animists. They believed that both animate, or living, things and inanimate objects were imbued with spirits and should be treated with respect. By the seventh century A.D., two Asian religions, Hinduism and Buddhism, were being practiced in the archipelago. The rituals of these religions were often blended with indigenous animist beliefs and with each other.

Hinduism is an ancient Indian religion. Hindus believe that a soul passes through many different stages of animal and human life until it finally attains enlightenment. Buddhism, a religion founded in India that was historically linked with Hinduism, is based on the idea that knowledge and the extinction of desire will lead one to nirvana, or enlightenment.

Some scholars believe the Brahmins, learned members of India's highest Hindu caste, had a significant role in bringing the religions of India to Indonesia. These experts believe the Brahmins were invited to Java and Sumatra as spiritual advisors by local rulers to elevate the rulers' status among their subjects. Other scholars cite Indonesia's geographic location as a major factor behind the arrival of Hinduism and Buddhism. Because of Indonesia's strategic location on the sea route between India and China, Hindu traders from south India and Chinese students of Buddhism traveling to India, introduced their religious ideas to the archipelago.

The first major Buddhist kingdom was the Srivijaya in Sumatra. In the seventh century A.D., Srivijaya became a strong sea power on the Strait of Malacca between Sumatra and the Malay Peninsula. Based in Palembang, the kingdom controlled much of the trade in Southeast Asia and established control over most of Sumatra, western Java, and parts of the Malay Peninsula. Palembang became a center of trade for merchants from Persia, Arabia, and India who exchanged goods such as frankincense and myrrh from the Middle East for silks, porcelain, and medical products from China. Indonesians traded precious woods and spices from the Maluku islands. The coastal kingdom was also a leading Buddhist center and attracted thousands of pilgrims and scholars from Asia. By the second half of the seventh century, local boatbuilders were constructing the largest ships in the world. Srivijaya dominated the Strait of Malacca and Chinese-Indian trade until the 11th century.

During the early eighth century, the Hindu Mataram dynasty gained control over the inland plains in Central Java, but Mataram power declined as the Buddhist Sailendra dynasty began to flourish from about 750 to 850. Between 778 and 850, the Sailendras built Borobudhur, a magnificent stone Buddhist monument, considered one of the great works of world religious art. In the ninth century Prambanan, a vast temple complex, was also built. However, Borobudhur and Prambanan were abandoned by the end of the tenth century, as stronger Hindu states emerged in eastern Java.

During the centuries that Buddhism and Hinduism were the major influences on Indonesia's culture and civilization, the last great power in Java was the Majapahit Empire, founded in East Java in 1294. The Majapahits conquered Srivijaya and by the 1300s controlled much of the archipelago. The empire reached its pinnacle of power during the middle of the 14th century under the rule of Hayam Wuruk and his prime minister, Gajah Mada. Under these leaders, trade thrived with much of the rest of the Indonesian region and the Malay Peninsula.

Majapahit power declined in the 14th and 15th centuries. The kingdom was weakened by internal problems and threatened by new states gaining power on the coast. The kingdom of Demak, a seaport on Java's northern coast and the capital of the first Javanese Islamic state, conquered Majapahit in 1478, although the final collapse of the Hindu-Buddhist state did not occur until 1527.

The Spread of Islam to Indonesia

The word *Islam* is derived from the Arabic verb *aslama*, which means "surrender." Followers of the religion are called to surrender to the will of the one God, or Allah. They believe that the teachings of Islam were revealed in A.D. 610 by the angel Gabriel to the prophet Muhammad, while he was meditating in a cave on the Arabian Peninsula. Muhammad later shared the revelations with others, and his teaching became the basis of the new religion. By the time Muhammad died in 632, most of the people of the Arabian Peninsula had converted to Islam.

Within 100 years of the prophet's death, Arab armies had spread the new religion to Spain and across the Middle East to Asia. By the ninth century, thousands of Muslim merchants from Guangzhou, China, had contact with Indonesia as they used the sea routes through the archipelago to conduct their trade.

In *A History of Modern Indonesia Since c. 1200*, M. C. Ricklefs writes, "The spread of Islam is one of the most significant processes of Indonesian history, but also one of the most obscure. Muslim traders had apparently been present in some parts of Indonesia for several centuries before Islam became established within the local communities." According to Ricklefs, there are no definite answers to how, when, and why Indonesians converted to Islam because few records of that period survive. It is thought that Arabs, Indians, Chinese, and other Asians who were already Muslims settled in Indonesia, intermarried with non-Muslims, and were assimilated into Indonesian life. While historians are unsure about the specific causes, there is a general consensus that Islam spread through Indonesia, in the words of Theodore Friend, "more by trade than by sword."

The first evidence of an early Islamic kingdom was a gravestone found in North Sumatra. The grave belonged to a **sultan**, or Muslim ruler, who died in 1211. In 1292, the Venetian merchant and explorer Marco Polo stopped in Sumatra on his return from China and reported that there were Muslim converts in the northern port of Perlak. It is thought that Muslim merchants stayed in the island's coastal towns while waiting for good sailing weather. Because these merchants figured importantly into the economy, local rulers most likely became their allies and found it advantageous to convert to Islam. The state of Aceh (also spelled *Atjeh*), founded in the early 16th century on the northern tip of the island, became one of the most influential Islamic regions in Indonesia.

Islamic gravestones found in East Java support the theory that the royalty of this area converted to Islam before their subjects did. It is possible that the educated Hindu-Buddhist elite and royalty were attracted to Sufism, the mystical teachings of Islam. Once the royalty converted, the people they ruled generally adopted the religion of their leaders.

The dome of a Muslim mosque on Ambon Island. Islam may have spread to Indonesia as early as the ninth century, just a few centuries after the death of the Prophet Muhammad in 632.

During the 16th century Islam spread from the important western trading areas to the eastern Maluku islands. Although there is little evidence of the practice of Islam during this period in other areas of the archipelago, it is likely that Muslims lived in many regions. There was resistance to conversion on the island of Bali, however, and to this day most of the inhabitants of Bali are Hindu rather than Muslim.

The European Colonial Period

At the beginning of the 15th century, Islamic states had an important role in the world, while the influence of Europe was less prominent. However, Europeans were making advances in the areas of geography and astronomy. The Portuguese in particular adopted knowledge and technology from Arab scholars and used them to begin a series of seafaring voyages along the coast of Africa. Explorers benefited from these technological improvements by finding ways to sail increasingly farther distances. During his 1497–99 journey, Portuguese explorer Vasco da Gama became the first person to sail from Europe around the Cape of Good Hope on the southern tip of Africa to India.

Gama's voyage was momentous, as it opened a direct trade route for Europeans to the Far East. During this period, Muslim merchants had established a trading center in Venice, Italy, and had a monopoly on the spice trade and imports to Europe. Spices were a valuable commodity—they were crucial not only for seasoning, but most importantly, for the preservation of meat. One highly prized spice was the clove from eastern Indonesia's Spice Islands, a region that also produced pepper, nutmeg, and mace. The Portuguese had become determined to bypass the Muslim traders and establish themselves in the spice trade.

In 1509 the Portuguese king, intent on monopolizing the spice trade of the eastern part of the archipelago, sent a party to Maluku, a thriving center of trade on the Malay Peninsula, as Portugal's representative to the East. The influential Muslim trading community of Maluku convinced their sultan that the Europeans were a threat and had them expelled. But the Portuguese returned in 1511, this time in force, and conquered Maluku.

The Portuguese remained in the archipelago for less than a century (except in East Timor, where they stayed until 1976). As a result of a lack of resources and organization, they were unable to hold on to the Asian spice trade. By the early 17th century, the Netherlands had supplanted Portugal as the European power that controlled the region.

The Netherlands had become an important commercial power in northern Europe, but they were under pressure to develop new overseas trade routes. In 1596, four Dutch ships arrived in Bantan, the center of the pepper trade on West Java. After clashing with the Portuguese and the Indonesians, the Dutch left empty-handed. The expedition then sailed to other ports on Java, this time with better results. Three ships returned to the Netherlands carrying enough spices to make the trip an economic success.

Over the next few years several Dutch trading companies made trips to Indonesia in search of spices. This was known as the period of "wild" voyages, during which rival companies vied for control of trade. To regulate competition, a group of Dutch traders formed the Dutch East India Company (VOC) in 1602. Under a charter issued by the government, the VOC was granted the power to wage war, build fortresses, and enter into treaty negotiations in Asia on behalf of the Netherlands.

In 1619 Jan Pieterszoon Coen became the governor-general of the VOC. This ambitious Dutchman, who held office during the years 1619–23 and 1627–29, was determined to establish a Dutch monopoly in the region. He erected trading posts and forts along the coast of Java and captured and destroyed its capital, Jakarta. On its site he built a new capital called Batavia that was inspired by Dutch architecture. By the end of the 17th century, the Dutch controlled most of the archipelago.

The VOC was ruthless in maintaining control of the spice trade, but over the next century its profits began to decline, and by December 1799

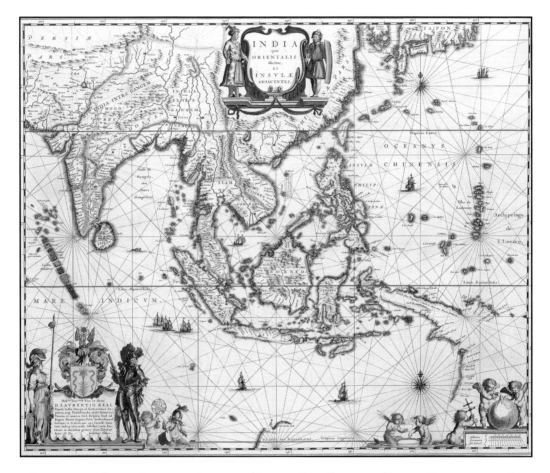

This map of southeast Asia was drawn by the noted Dutch cartographer Willem Blaeu in the early 17th century.

it was bankrupt. The Netherlands abolished the VOC by letting its charter lapse, after which the company's territory was declared a Dutch colony called the Dutch East Indies.

Two years later, Herman Willem Daendels became governor-general of the Dutch possessions. He was appointed by the ruler of the Netherlands, Louis Bonaparte, brother of the French emperor Napoleon. Both leaders at the time were contending with Britain and its allies during a series of conflicts known as the Napoleonic Wars. Daendels opposed the oppressiveness of the system that existed in the colony and introduced reforms.

However, his agenda was interrupted by British advances on Indonesia. The ensuing battles in 1810–11, together known as the Anglo-Dutch Java War, ended in British victory. The British East India Company occupied Java and took temporary control of Indonesia from the Netherlands.

Under British rule, Sir Thomas Stamford Raffles was made lieutenant governor-general of Java. He too attempted liberal reforms, such as abolishing the slave trade in the archipelago and letting the peasants decide which crops to grow. But in 1816, after the Napoleonic Wars ended, Dutch authority was reestablished in the region.

The Java War and the Cultivation System

Years of colonial exploitation, poor harvests, and high taxes fueled popular support for the Java War (1825–30). Pangeran Diponegoro, a prince and a student of Islam who had a strong following among the Muslim community and the rural masses, led this guerrilla revolt against the Dutch. Over 200,000 Javanese and thousands of other Indonesians and Dutch were killed in the war, which ended in the guerrillas' defeat. After the war the Dutch forced peasants to grow large amounts of export crops, especially sugar, coffee, and indigo, for the government instead of letting them cultivate their land for much-needed rice. As a result, famines and rice shortages were widespread.

The Dutch colonial government often faced opposition from Sumatran rulers who retained control of certain regions of the archipelago. The Padri War (1821–38) was initiated by religious teachers intent on ridding North Sumatra's Minangkabau region of non-Islamic customs such as gambling, cock fighting, the use of alcohol and opium, and aspects of the local law. The resulting clash between the religious group and the secular leaders led to the intervention of the Dutch, who pacified the region. During the Aceh War (1873–1904), one of the bloodiest and longest in Dutch or Indonesian history, the Netherlands fought for and won control of the Islamic region of Aceh.

The Beginnings of Nationalism

By the end of the 19th century the Dutch approach toward Indonesia began to shift from that of exploitation toward concern for the people's well-being. This new viewpoint was sparked in part by the publication of a popular novel titled *Max Havelaar* (1860), which exposed the oppression of the Javanese peasants and alerted many Europeans to problems in the region. In 1899 Conrad Theodoor van Deventer, a lawyer who had lived in Indonesia, published an article titled "A Debt of Honor" in a Dutch journal. In the essay he argued that the Dutch had a moral responsibility to repay the Indonesians for all of the profits that had been made from the exploitation of their country. In 1901 his ideas became the basis for the Netherlands's Ethical Policy, which promoted education, irrigation, and emigration from overcrowded Java to less populated islands.

The Dutch began to improve the infrastructure, health-care system, and education of Indonesians during the early 1900s. Although some promised changes were never made, there were still major developments, including the additions of several newspapers, railroads, factories, and hotels. Members of the privileged class were offered the opportunity to study in Europe, while others started successful businesses. Despite the reforms, members of Java's intellectual and business elite eventually resented colonial rule enough to start the first Indonesian nationalist organizations.

An important early movement was Sarekat Islam (Islamic Union, or SI), organized in 1912 to help Indonesian **batik** merchants compete with the growing Chinese trade. By 1919 the group, headquartered in Java, had a membership of some 500,000. Despite its name, the organization did not have deep religious roots, though in maintaining an exclusive Muslim membership it distinguished itself from the Dutch and Chinese competition. By early 1927, SI had ceased to operate, though other groups would pick up where it left off.

As the Dutch tightened their hold, secular nationalist movements intensified. On July 4, 1927, the Indonesian Nationalist Party was founded and headed by Sukarno (many Indonesians only have one name). Sukarno (1901–1970) was an educated Indonesian who believed that establishing an independent, secular state should be the foremost goal of Indonesians.

Sukarno and other nationalist leaders were arrested and exiled several times, and the Dutch banned various nationalist parties. Despite these crackdowns, the movement continued to grow. An Indonesian language of national unity was adopted during this period. Called Bahasa Indonesia,

This Dutch colonial-style building, guarded by cannons, was part of Fort De Kock, a Dutch settlement on Sumatra.

Laborers make diagonal cuts into rubber trees to extract the valuable sap. The Dutch exploited the rubber and other resources of their Indonesian colony.

it was based on the Malay language that had been used for centuries in the archipelago and was not connected to any specific ethnic group.

Indonesia suffered during the worldwide economic depression of the 1930s. It lost its century-old position as the leading exporter of sugar and coffee. At the same time, the Dutch began discontinuing their liberal reforms and rejected all Indonesian negotiations for self-rule. One Dutch governor-general is alleged to have said, "The Dutch have been here for 350 years with stick and sword and will remain another 350 years with stick and sword."

But this was not to be. After the Japanese attacked Pearl Harbor on December 7, 1941, the United States declared war on Japan, entering World War II. The Japanese felt they should control the territories of the Pacific Ocean, and sought to capture Western possessions, such as the U.S.-controlled Philippines, the British colonies of Malaya and Singapore, and the Dutch East Indies. On January 10, 1942, Japanese forces invaded Indonesia and destroyed an Allied fleet in the Battle of the Java Sea. The Indonesians gave little military help to the Dutch, and on March 8, 1942, Dutch authorities on Java surrendered to Japan. The governor-general was arrested, and eventually most Europeans in the area were sent to internment camps.

The Japanese Occupation

At first, the Indonesians viewed the Japanese as liberators, but the Japanese regime proved to be harsh and repressive. To continue its war effort, Japan needed Indonesia's resources. In the interest of garnering support, they backed the Muslims and nationalists and freed Sukarno from exile. But the Japanese were also ruthless in their exploitation of Indonesian labor. At least 200,000 men were forced to leave their villages in Java and work as slaves in Burma (now Myanmar) and Siam (now Thailand), many never to return.

Sukarno, who was retained by the Japanese to help them govern, saw an opportunity to spread his doctrine of secular nationalism. On August 15, 1945, Japan was forced to surrender to the Allies and its reign in Indonesia ended. Two days later, Sukarno read a simple declaration of independence to a small group of people in front of his house in Jakarta. Sukarno and Mohammad Hatta (1902–1980) were selected, respectively, as the first president and vice president of the new Republic of Indonesia. August 17 became Indonesia's national Independence Day.

Struggle for Independence

British and Dutch forces landed in Indonesia in September 1945 to round up and disarm the Japanese. When the British left in November 1946 there were 55,000 Dutch troops in Java. The British convinced the Dutch and the Indonesians to sign the Linggajati Agreement, under which the Netherlands would recognize the republic and set the stage for a federal Indonesia as part of a Dutch commonwealth. But in July 1947 the Dutch violated the agreement and the military attacked several key cities on Java and Sumatra, killing thousands. In response, Indonesian nationalists attacked Dutch targets.

The attacks provoked international opposition, convincing the United Nations (U.N.) to form a Good Offices Commission that oversaw the signing of the Renville Agreement (1948). The agreement proclaimed a truce between the Netherlands and the Republic of Indonesia, though anti-Dutch sentiment continued to grow.

Yogyakarta, the temporary capital, was bombed and occupied by Dutch troops in December 1948 and Sukarno and other top leaders were arrested. Around this time, it was discovered that the amount the Dutch were spending to regain the islands and destroy the nationalist movement was close to the amount of money the United States had given the Netherlands under the Marshall Plan for war reconstruction aid. In an

Dutch troops carry out operations against Indonesian nationalists in Magelang, Java, 1949. The Dutch fought to regain control of their colony until the United Nations stepped in to negotiate Indonesia's independence.

effort to force the Netherlands to withdraw, the United States halted its financial support.

Under increasing international pressure, and aware that it would be difficult to defeat the republic's popular resistance movement, the Netherlands agreed to grant independence to all of Indonesia except Irian Jaya (for the next 20 years, this region remained under the control of the Netherlands, and later the U.N.). On December 27, 1949, the Republic of Indonesia was formally established and the Dutch East Indies ceased to exist.

The Sukarno Years

On the day of the nation's new independence, shouts of *Merdeka, merdeka!* ("Freedom, freedom!") were heard throughout Indonesia as flag-waving crowds celebrated. But the fledgling country was faced with many deep-rooted problems. Indonesia was an impoverished nation. The largely illiterate population was growing at an extraordinary rate. Plantations and

Nationalist leader Sukarno (1901–1970) declared Indonesia's independence on August 17, 1945, and became the country's first president.

factories were damaged or closed, and food, money, and skilled workers were in short supply.

Dutch-educated nationalists and Islamic parties agreed to create a unified, Western-style parliamentary state. But across the archipelago differences in thinking produced more than 30 parties, of which the four largest were variously based on the principles of Islam, nationalism, or communism. Separatist movements and uprisings divided the new Indonesian republic. Darul Islam (Islamic Domain), a militant group in West Java, believed in an Islamic state and fought the government from 1948 to 1962. There were also revolts in southern Sulawesi and Aceh, where Darul Islam had taken hold.

To resolve the internal conflicts, Sukarno imposed martial law and allowed the Indonesian military to suppress rebels paramilitary and political groups. Gradually, Sukarno's nationalist party joined forces with the Indonesian Communist Party (PKI). In 1957, the PKI and nationalist party unions began taking over Dutch businesses. On December 5, 1957, the Ministry of Justice expelled about 46,000 Dutch citizens from Indonesia. The issue of Irian Jaya was finally settled in 1962 when the Dutch agreed to transfer the region to the U.N., which turned it over to

Indonesia on May 1, 1963. In 1969, Irian Jaya became Indonesia's 26th province.

In 1959, Sukarno introduced a more authoritarian policy called Guided Democracy that gave most of the power to the president and the military. However, Sukarno's extravagant construction of new stadiums and monuments could not hide the corruption, poverty, and economic instability that marred the country.

Internationally, though, Indonesia began to play an important role in world affairs. In April 1955 Sukarno hosted the Asian-African Conference at Bandung, West Java, which brought together 29 nations for the largest non-Western conference of the postwar period. The Bandung Conference promoted cooperation between developing countries that were not aligned with either the United States or Russia in the Cold War. The conference boosted Indonesia's status as a leader of the non-aligned nations (sometimes called the "third world" countries).

On September 16, 1963, the former British colonies of Malaya, Singapore, Sabah, and Sarawak united to form the nation of Malaysia. Because Sukarno perceived continued British influence in Malaysia, he opposed the creation of this new country. Declaring that Indonesia would "crush Malaysia," Sukarno began a political, economic, and military confrontation with the new nation. When the U.N. made Malaysia a member in 1964, Sukarno pulled Indonesia out of the international organization, which it had joined in 1950.

This external tension, along with internal corruption, contributed to hard times. From 1961 to 1964 annual inflation hovered at 100 percent or more, foreign investors withdrew, food shortages abounded, and rivalries between various factions grew. Rebel movements spread as people on the outer islands felt that Java was given preferential treatment. President Sukarno allied himself more with the PKI, whose membership of 2 million made it the world's largest communist party in a non-communist country.

The 1965 Coup and Its Aftermath

On the night of September 30, 1965, six top generals were assassinated by a group of young officers who claimed the generals were plotting a coup to take over the government. General Suharto (also spelled Soeharto), then head of the elite Army Strategic Reserve, mobilized the army and quickly defeated the officers' revolt.

Suharto and the army claimed that the officers were attempting a communist coup. A violent anticommunist purge ensued. On Bali and throughout the country, the army and Muslim groups killed hundreds of thousands of suspected communists and arrested still more. Some suspected the Chinese of supporting the coup; they were already targeted as scapegoats because of their financial success and their status as foreigners.

However, even today experts are divided about the extent of the danger. Some scholars assert that the coup was an internal army affair, instigated by Suharto in a play for power. Others consider the counter-coup to be a response to an actual communist uprising, or the inevitable outcome of cultural war in Java.

Sukarno's authority diminished after the revolt, and he signed an executive order that gave ultimate power to Suharto on March 11, 1966. The PKI was officially banned on March 13, 1966. Suharto was installed a year later as acting president, and officially inaugurated as president in 1968, while Sukarno was kept under house arrest until his death in June 1970.

Suharto's New Order

Unlike Sukarno, Suharto was receptive to Western ideas and recruited Western-educated economists to assist in setting new financial policy. He established a New Order government that encouraged foreign investment; instituted a successful family planning program; made educational advances; and raised the standard of living for many Indonesians.

However, during his more than 30 years in power Suharto led a **hierarchical** regime, in which the military and police played a powerful central role.

In 1966, Indonesia rejoined the U.N. and the International Monetary Fund. Indonesia also became a founding member of the Association of Southeast Asian Nations (ASEAN), established in 1967.

In 1969 Suharto instituted the first in a series of Five-Year Development Plans, involving government investment in agriculture, economic infrastructure, and import-export industries. To attain much-needed western economic aid, he ended the confrontation with Malaysia.

Oil was the centerpiece of the country's economic policy by the late 1960s. In 1968 Indonesia's two oil companies merged into one enterprise

Sukarno had not aligned Indonesia with either the Soviet Union or the United States during the Cold War; however, by the mid-1960s some people feared Indonesia was leaning toward communism. In 1965 Indonesian general Suharto (pictured) used an alleged communist takeover of the government as an opportunity to seize power. Sukarno gave up the presidency to Suharto on March 11, 1966.

called Pertamina. Oil production grew, and after the Arab-Israeli War in October 1973, oil prices shot up. But despite the high price of oil, Indonesia was still the poorest and most populated member of the Organization of Petroleum Exporting Countries (OPEC). In 1975 the government was forced to take control of Pertamina in order to repay the troubled company's outstanding loans.

A year after a 1974 revolution in Portugal overthrew that country's military dictatorship, the Portuguese withdrew from their colony of East Timor. Fretilin, a leftist group on the island, immediately declared independence. The government in Jakarta, opposed to an independent state within its archipelago, invaded East Timor on December 7, 1975. By July 1976, following the execution of an estimated 60,000 civilians, East Timor was forcibly incorporated as Indonesia's 27th province.

A period of economic prosperity during the 1970s created a new middle class; it also made the poor better off and increased the fortunes of the rich. Corruption and **nepotism** were rampant in the Suharto regime, but these problems were largely ignored by Indonesians and foreign investors as profits increased. By 1981 Indonesia had become the world's largest producer of liquefied natural gas, rice production was up, and tourism—especially on Bali—brought in foreign dollars. By 1982, the World Bank had classified Indonesia as a middle-income country, despite falling oil prices and a large foreign debt.

Suharto was given the title "Father of Development" by parliamentary decree in 1983. Under his leadership, generous foreign investment resulted in the growth of industry, manufacturing, and infrastructure. By the mid-1980s, thanks to technological advances, government policy, and the hard work of its people, Indonesia became self-sufficient in rice production. During this period literacy rates were increasing and by 1990 over 80 percent of Indonesians over the age of five could speak Bahasa Indonesia. In addition, the country had one of the most successful family planning programs in the world. Population growth fell from 2.32 percent in the 1960s to 1.97 percent in the 1980s.

But these promising developments were overshadowed by two negative factors. First, the increased development was financed by loans from Japan and the United States. In 1982, when oil prices began to fall, Indonesia's debt was almost $21 billion; by 1988 it had risen to over $51 billion. Second, the growth of foreign investment created new opportunities for corruption. Internationally, Indonesia was generally considered to be the most corrupt nation in the world by the early 1990s. Bribes and kickbacks were commonplace throughout the government. Suharto and his family and friends controlled businesses across the country. Through special contracts and favoritism, Suharto's children owned gas and oil ventures, toll roads, taxi fleets, skyscrapers, hotels, and more. This corruption eventually led to political discontent.

In July 1997 the growth of foreign investment came to an abrupt, almost total halt, as the Asian financial crisis that had begun in Thailand hit Indonesia. Foreign investors lost faith in Indonesia's economy and refused to finance further investment. The rupiah, Indonesia's currency, became almost worthless, banks collapsed, the stock market plummeted, prices skyrocketed, and over 14 million people lost their jobs. The savings of the new middle class dissolved, as virtually every major business in the country went bankrupt.

Suharto was up for reelection in February 1998, but he faced massive dissent from students, Muslim parties, and others opposed to his policies and the corruption of his regime. There were demonstrations on university campuses. In April, rioting erupted in Medan, Sumatra, and spread to other cities, in part because fuel prices had increased over 70 percent.

During a protest held on May 12, 1998, soldiers shot and killed four students at Trisakti University in Jakarta. The city exploded in rioting and looting that lasted over four days. Over 1,200 people died and over 6,000 buildings were damaged or destroyed. On May 18, the speaker of the People's Consultative Assembly (MPR) publicly asked the president to resign in the interests of the country. On May 21, after 32 years in power, Suharto agreed to step down.

Vice President B. J. Habibie was promptly sworn in as Indonesia's third president. He introduced democratic reforms, including the promise of elections in 1999. However, Habibie faced a disastrous economy with 56 percent of the population below the poverty level. In addition, for 15 years there had been increasing levels of ethnic, religious, and separatist violence and Islamic fervor throughout the archipelago.

In May 1999 the U.N. set a date for a referendum in East Timor. This vote offered the people a choice between *autonomy*—remaining a part of Indonesia but having a large measure of self-government—and complete independence. On August 30, 1999, 98.6 percent of the East Timorese turned out at the polls; 78.5 percent voted for independence, and 21.5 percent voted for an autonomous state. Instead of accepting the outcome, the Indonesian militia unleashed a reign of violence in which thousands of East Timorese were killed and 800,000 became refugees. Following the attacks, which received international condemnation, armed U.N. peacekeepers and 2,500 troops from six countries under Australian command went into East Timor to restore order. On May 20, 2002, East Timor was recognized as an independent nation after years of struggle.

Abdurrahman Wahid and Megawati Sukarnoputri

While the fighting was occurring over East Timor, Indonesia held its first free parliamentary election in 40 years. Ninety-three percent of Indonesia's registered voters cast their ballots on June 7, 1999. Despite a growing interest in Islam, most voters supported secular parties. Megawati Sukarnoputri's Indonesian Democratic Party of Struggle (PDI-P) emerged in the lead, but when representatives in the People's Consultative Assembly (MPR) met to vote in October, electors from several parties united to elect Abdurrahman Wahid, a popular leader of a very large Muslim organization. With Wahid as Indonesia's fourth president, Megawati, Sukarno's daughter, was made vice president.

Wahid, popularly known as Gus Dur, began his presidency determined to reform the crippling governmental bureaucracy and stem corruption in the marketplace. Overall, however, he did little to eradicate the nation's many problems. During his term there was increasing religious, ethic, and separatist violence. Wahid's presidency, marred by chaos and incompetence, came to an end in July 2001 when the MPR removed him from power and installed Megawati as Indonesia's fifth president.

As president, Megawati was criticized for passively allowing the democratic reforms begun in 1998 to develop slowly. During her time in office, economic conditions worsened for ordinary Indonesians and the health care and educational systems continued to stagnate. By early 2004 it was clear that her popularity among Indonesians had fallen.

In July 2004 Megawati finished second in a multi-candidate race for the presidency, ahead of several candidates but behind Susilo Bambang Yudhoyono, a former general who had been security minister in Megawati's administration. Because no candidate received a clear majority, the top two vote-getters participated in a runoff election in September. Yudhoyono won by a wide margin, receiving about 61 percent of the vote to Megawati's 39 percent. The voting was carried out peacefully, and foreign monitors pronounced it "free and fair."

The 2004 presidential election was notable because it was the first time Indonesian voters chose their leader directly. Yudhoyono took office in October, promising that as president he would crack down on terrorism in the archipelago, take steps to improve the economy, and curb corruption in government.

Indonesians work on the assembly line of an automobile manu-facturing plant in Jakarta. Thanks to a surplus of low-cost labor, industry is a growing sector of Indonesia's economy.

4

The Economy, Politics, and Religion

Indonesia's natural resources are among the richest in the world, though the country plays only a modest role in the global economy. The country's major markets for exports are Japan, Singapore, Taiwan, Korea, the European Union (EU), and the United States. Major suppliers of imports are Japan, the United States, and Thailand.

Although industry and manufacturing are growing sectors of the economy, Indonesia still primarily supplies raw materials to international markets. It mainly imports chemicals, consumer goods, and some foods. Indonesia's government owns over 164 enterprises and sets the prices on various basic supplies including fuel, rice, and electricity. Oil, natural gas, timber products (including plywood), minerals, and manufactured goods are major exports and an important source of revenue. Large estates produce almost all of the agricultural commodities for export, which include coffee, tobacco, tea, spices, and palm oil.

Agriculture accounts for only 16 percent of Indonesia's **gross domestic product (GDP)**, but almost half of the labor force is involved in agricultural enterprises, either as independent peasant farmers or on large estates. The estates cover a total area of approximately 1.6 million acres (6.6 million hectares) and are mainly located on Sumatra, home of many rubber plantations, and East Java, where tobacco is cultivated.

Rice is a staple of the Indonesian diet and an important part of peasant agriculture. In the 1970s the government introduced new varieties of rice, advanced forms of irrigation and fertilization, and price controls that ended Indonesia's dependence on rice imports. The crop is grown mainly on Java and the western islands, where over 90 percent of the farmers live.

Farmers on Java, Bali, and Lombok still use the ancient *sawah* method of wet rice cultivation. This complex system is especially suited to highland areas, where fields are cleared and then terraced with intricate irrigation systems. Often maintained through local cooperatives, this system can yield two or more rice crops a year. In the less fertile areas a small percentage of farmers still practice a slash-and-burn method of agriculture. Unfortunately, this leads to the destruction of forests; as the soil ultimately becomes less fertile, the farmers must move on and repeat the process.

Indonesia is the only Asian country that is a member of the Organization of Petroleum Exporting Countries (OPEC). The country ranks 17th among oil-producing nations with approximately 1.9 percent of the world's production. The first commercial oil well in Indonesia was established in North Sumatra in 1883. Today, there are offshore sites in the Java Sea, but most oil comes from Sumatra and Kalimantan. Pertamina, the national oil company, controls all rights to oil and gas production. It is scheduled to become a private company in 2006.

Oil exports are a mainstay of the nation's export earnings. However, Indonesia's oil wells are drying up and new fields have yet to be discovered. With the internal demand for fuel growing, new oil reserves will need to be tapped or Indonesia will eventually import more oil than it exports.

In the 1980s Indonesia began to enlarge its manufacturing base. Today many of the largest industries are state-owned and process mineral and agricultural products. There are also medium- and small-scale privately owned businesses that produce footwear, chemicals, wood products, glassware, and cement, among other goods. Automobiles, trucks, and motorcycles are assembled in Indonesian factories under license from foreign manufacturers,

A tanker ship is loaded with oil at a refinery near Balikpapan. Indonesia has access to a large reserve of oil, and is the only Asian country to be a member of the oil cartel OPEC.

as are electronic equipment and appliances. Most industrial plants are located on Java, with Jakarta and Surabaya the main manufacturing centers. The industrial sector accounts for 42 percent of Indonesia's GDP, and employs 16 percent of the labor force.

Indonesia has a wealth of minerals, and many geologists believe the islands have vast undiscovered resources as well. The nation is the world's third-largest producer of tin. What may be one of the largest nickel deposits in the world is located in eastern Indonesia on sparsely inhabited Gag Island. Many of the country's largest copper and gold deposits are also located in the remote eastern islands. Bauxite from the Riau Islands and West Kalimantan is processed into aluminum at a smelter in North Sumatra, the first aluminum smelter built in Southeast Asia. East and South Kalimantan have major coal excavation sites.

New mining investment, however, has dramatically decreased in recent years and some companies have left Indonesia, as attempts to give more power to provincial and local governments have disrupted industry regulation. Widespread lawlessness and unclear tax rules are among the problems that worry investors. A 2003 survey by PricewaterhouseCoopers noted that spending on mineral exploration fell from $160 million in 1996 to $19 million in 2002. Until the problems are resolved, mining industry leaders do not believe Indonesia will attract a sufficient number of new investors.

Timber, especially teak and other hardwoods, is another important Indonesian export. The archipelago has one of the world's largest expanses of tropical forests, which cover more than 60 percent of the country. Approximately two-thirds of the forests—particularly those on Kalimantan and Sumatra—are used for commercial enterprises. The timber industry has expanded rapidly since 1960, and this has often resulted in the over-cutting of trees and environmental damage. In an effort to protect large forest areas, the government has begun reforestation programs and banned exports of raw logs, although neither course of action has been effective to date.

The Economy of Indonesia

Gross domestic product (GDP*): $172.9 billion (2002)

Per capita income: $796 (2002)

Inflation: 6.9%

Natural resources: petroleum, natural gas, tin, nickel, timber, bauxite, copper, fertile soils, coal, gold, silver

Industry (42.1% of GDP): petroleum and natural gas, textiles, apparel, footwear, mining, cement, chemical fertilizers, plywood, rubber, food, tourism (2002 est.)

Agriculture (15.9% of GDP): rice, cassava (tapioca), peanuts, rubber, cocoa, coffee, palm oil, copra, poultry, beef, pork, eggs (2002 est.)

Services (42% of GDP): communications, transportation, shipping (2001 est.)

Foreign trade:

    Imports: $40.22 billion—machinery and equipment, chemicals, fuels, foodstuffs

    Exports: $63.89 billion—oil and gas, electrical appliances, plywood, textiles, rubber

Currency exchange rate: U.S. $1 = 9,225 Indonesian rupiah (2004)

*GDP, or gross domestic product, is the total value of goods and services produced in a country annually.

All figures are 2003 estimates unless otherwise noted.

Sources: U.S. Department of State; CIA World Factbook, 2004.

Fishing is a growing industry in Indonesia. With government assistance, fish production is increasing annually at an estimated rate of 5.4 percent. Shrimp and tuna are the most popular fish for export, and snails are shipped from Indonesia to Europe, where in certain countries they are considered a delicacy. The commercial fishing industry is based mostly in Java.

The tourist industry was one of the country's most rapidly developing business sectors until the Asian financial crisis in 1997. It was further hurt by a terrorist bomb attack at a Bali nightclub in October 2002, in which 202 people, mostly tourists, were killed, and a bombing outside a Marriott hotel in Jakarta in August 2003, in which 14 died. Tourism has slowly begun to revive and by early 2004 the number of foreigners arriving in the Bali airport was back to almost two-thirds the level before the nightclub bombing.

The service sector, which includes industries such as communications, transportation, and shipping, accounts for 42 percent of the GDP and employs 39 percent of the population. Since 1976 Indonesia has had its own communications satellite system, and this has led to the rapid growth of telephone, television, and broadcast facilities in all of the provinces. In 2000 there were 24 internet service providers and by 2002, there were 4.4 million internet users across the archipelago.

Indonesia was the hardest hit of all the Asian nations by the Asian financial crisis in 1997. Before the crisis an estimated 20 million people—11 percent of the population—lived below the poverty line, down from 40 percent in 1976. One year after the crisis, almost half the population—about 100 million Indonesians—had incomes below poverty level. However, the country's income numbers rebounded fairly quickly. By 1999 about 27 percent of the population was below the poverty line, and by mid-2003, Indonesia's economy had reached its pre-1997 GDP levels. Economists estimate that the national poverty level will be back down to about 11 percent by the end of 2005.

Efforts are being made to improve Indonesia's economy, but the task is huge and the pace of reform is slow. Potential foreign investors are concerned about terrorist threats, the decentralization of the government, corruption, regional ethnic and religious conflicts, and tax and labor issues. Experts believe that to undergo further economic growth, Indonesia must commit to internal reform, reestablishing the confidence of international donors and investors, and becoming an active player in the global economy.

Indonesia's Political System

Indonesia is an independent republic, and its 1945 constitution was drafted and adopted the year the country proclaimed independence from the Netherlands. This constitution was replaced in 1950, and later reinstated to bolster Sukarno's authoritarian powers in 1959. Since 1998, the constitution's amendments have allowed it to operate as the basis of democratic government.

The constitution is based on the state philosophy of **Pancasila**, which was introduced by Sukarno in 1945. The philosophy consists of five principles: belief in the "one and only God"; humanitarian practices; the unity of Indonesia; democratic government by consensus; and social justice for all Indonesians. In 1978, to maintain and encourage a unified nation, Suharto began to intensify promotion of Pancasila. Under Suharto, all citizens were required to study the tenets of the state philosophy in schools, the workplace, and government offices. Today, the message of Pancasila—namely the importance of national unity and common interests over ethnic and religious divisions—continues to be promoted, but without the dogmatic approach used during the Suharto years.

The president of Indonesia is both the head of state and chief executive. Until a 2002 amendment was made to the 1945 constitution, the president and vice president were elected separately by the Indonesian parliament to five-year terms. The amendment meant that in 2004, Indonesians voted directly for these leaders for the first time.

Indonesians may vote when they are 17 years old or if they are married, regardless of age. Voting is by secret ballot. Indonesians may run for office at 21 years of age.

Susilo Bambang Yudhoyono, elected president of Indonesia in September 2004, speaks at a press conference.

The president oversees administration of the government, rules by decree in emergencies, and has the supreme command of the army, navy, and air force. However, the president is accountable to the People's Consultative Assembly (MPR), the upper house of national parliament. The president appoints a cabinet that assists in executing administrative duties.

The parliament, which includes the MPR and the House of Representatives, or DPR, is the highest legislative institution in Indonesia. The legislative body also used to have the power to formulate national policy, along with voting for the president and vice-president, but now only meets annually to consider constitutional changes.

Members of the legislature serve five-year terms. They vote on all statutes and are able to submit draft bills for ratification by the president. The majority of the seats are elected by popular vote. Until recently, 38 seats were reserved for appointed members of the armed forces, but the military seats were eliminated in the April 2004 elections as part of an overall reduction of the military role in politics. Although the military is still an influential institution, military officials must now resign from the armed forces before assuming a government position.

After Suharto's resignation in 1998, there was a resurgence of political parties. Today, secular and nationalist ideologies underpin the two most prominent parties. One is the Indonesian Democratic Party of Struggle (PDI-P); the other is Golkar, which was founded by former president Suharto. There are several Islamic parties, including the National Awakening Party and the National Mandate Party of Amien Rais, a moderate Muslim intellectual. Those parties are affiliated, respectively, with the Nahdatul Ulama and the Muhammadiyah, moderate groups that are the country's largest Muslim organizations. Notable emerging parties include the newly formed Prosperous Justice Party, a small but growing Islamic party with a strong anti-corruption, pro-education message; and the new Democratic Party.

Indonesia's legal system is based on Roman-Dutch law, although it has been modified by indigenous beliefs and by a new criminal procedures code. The Supreme Court sits in Jakarta and is the final court of appeal. The court was restructured in 1968 to satisfy the conditions of the 1945 constitution and to be free from outside interference when administering justice. There are 51 members of the court. They are appointed by the president from a list prepared by the DPR.

The Supreme Court will soon take administrative responsibility for the country's lower courts, which are now run by the Ministry of Justice and Human Rights. Below the Supreme Court are the appellate courts, which are located in 14 major cities. There are also over 250 district courts that try criminal and civil cases. The criminal cases are tried under a unified code, but the civil cases are tried under **adat**, a customary law that varies from district to district or ethnic group. Westerners and Asians who are foreigners are tried under a European-based civil code. Unfortunately, justice in Indonesia is often influenced by bribes and behind-the-scenes deals.

Indonesia is divided into 32 provinces, two special regions (Aceh and Yogyakarta), and one special metropolitan district (Jakarta). The provinces are managed by governors who are appointed by the president under the advice of the Minister for Home Affairs and provincial parliaments. On January 1, 2001, a process of decentralization divided the provinces into 357 districts, or regencies, to act as key administrative units providing most government services. These districts were separated into 3,625 sub-districts that were then further divided into village groupings. Each layer has its own bureaucracy, and bureaucracies often overlap.

The village, or *desa,* is run by a grassroots administration of an elected (though sometimes hereditary) village head and a council of elders, composed of 9 to 15 distinguished village leaders. This framework of authority provides day-to-day support and guidance for local disputes and affairs. Two informal, voluntary organizations, the *Rukun Tetangga* and *Rukun Warga*, are in charge of neighborhood security, registration of families, and garbage collection, among other duties.

Issues of Human Rights and Corruption

A 2004 report by the international organization Human Rights Watch states that civil liberties have improved for most Indonesians since the Suharto regime ended in 1998. However, the report notes that important issues still remain, including the reemergence of the military in social and political affairs; the failure to sentence members of the security force responsible for past atrocities; and continuing abuses in Aceh and Irian Jaya.

A March 2004 *New York Times* article placed former president Suharto at the top of a list of leaders accused of embezzling large sums of money from their countries over the past 20 years. The article, which was based on a report compiled by Transparency International, estimates that Suharto allegedly stole $15 billion to $35 billion.

Suharto's New Order regime exercised tight restrictions on the media, and repressed critics of the government. Although it relaxed these restrictions briefly in the early 1990s, in 1994 the government banned three major publications, *Tempo, Editor,* and *Detik*—an act that, in the words of the international human-rights organization Amnesty International, "served to significantly inhibit media freedom and reverse the trend towards greater openness in reporting."

Following Suharto's resignation, the press was given greater latitude to operate, and Indonesia was soon considered a center of media freedom in Southeast Asia. However, in recent times there appears to have been an increase in media censorship. In 2003 and 2004, a series of cases brought against national newspapers, as well as the respected newsmagazine *Tempo,* threatened to shut down the publications. "Legal cases recently brought against media professionals highlight continuing flaws in the Indonesian legal system and indicate disturbing attempts to restrict fundamental rights to freedom of expression and opinion and the public's right to access to information," reported Amnesty International in October 2003.

In another case, in June 2004, the Indonesian government expelled the Jakarta-based chief of the International Crisis Group, an international advocacy organization which had been reporting on terrorism in Indonesia and the conflict in Aceh. This drew criticism from many outside governments and groups; a spokesman for the U.S. Department of State said the expulsion "would stand in stark contrast to the impressive progress made by Indonesia in recent years in developing a democratic civil society with freedom of expression."

Religion in Indonesia

Indonesia has the world's largest Muslim population, yet its constitution grants all Indonesians the right to practice other religions freely. Approximately 88 percent of the population is Muslim, 5 percent Protestant Christian, 3 percent Roman Catholic, 2 percent Hindu, 1 percent Buddhist, and 1 percent undefined. Although the census does not include animism in its figures, in some remote regions this is still practiced.

Although Pancasila endorses "belief in the one and only God," the government promotes religious tolerance. The state provides funds to build houses of worship for all religions (though chiefly for Islam), and according to a government publication, thousands are built every year. The government also provides financial assistance for Muslims traveling to Mecca, Saudi Arabia. Approximately 100,000 Indonesians make the **hajj**, or ritual pilgrimage, each year.

In addition to public schools, the state runs public Islamic schools from elementary through high school level, as well as 14 Islamic Religious Institutes and the State Islamic University in Jakarta. There are also private religious schools throughout the country.

Indonesia contains three-fourths as many Muslims as the populations of all Arab countries combined, yet in most areas Islamic practice is not as strict as in some Middle Eastern nations. From ancient times, many Indonesians have fused their religious beliefs in a **syncretistic** manner: animism blended into Hinduism and Buddhism, which was eventually absorbed by Islam. This layering of belief systems helps explain the less-severe interpretation of Islam and the religious tolerance practiced in Indonesia. At a 2002 conference entitled "Islam in Modern Indonesia," sponsored by the United States–Indonesia Society and the Asia Foundation, speaker Azyumardi Azra explained that because of the "slow, peaceful penetration" of the religion in Indonesia over time, and "because of the less rigid structure of Indonesian traditional society (including the active role of women in public life), the conventional wisdom of Indonesian Islam as tolerant, inclusive and inherently compatible with democracy is valid."

In Indonesia women have somewhat more freedom than their counterparts in many other Islamic countries. Traditional customs as well as Islamic and modern influences all affect the status of Indonesian women. Although women are regarded primarily as homemakers, they are an active part of the workforce and are not segregated from men. A minority chooses to wear the *hijab*, or Muslim head covering. Women are allowed to initiate divorce proceedings, whereas in some other Muslim countries it is the sole right of men. **Polygamy** is uncommon in Indonesia, although it is allowed under the 1974 Indonesian Marriage Law for religions that permit it (Islam, Buddhism, and Hinduism). Men are allowed to marry more than one wife, as long as they receive the permission of their wife or wives.

Most Muslims in Indonesia practice a tolerant and liberal interpretation of Islam, although they share the same basic rituals and practices of the faith with Muslims in the rest of the world. Most Indonesian Muslims observe traditional

This large gong—a reminder of Southeast Asia's pre-Islamic past—is used to accompany the standard Muslim call to prayer at the Masjid Agung mosque in Dernak.

rituals of Islam such as Ramadan, the month-long fast that occurs in the ninth month of the Islamic calendar. During this holiday Muslims eat breakfast before dawn and then fast until sundown. Observant Muslims also try to make the pilgrimage to Mecca once in their lifetime. Five times a day the *muezzin*, or criers, call the devout to prayer from the **mosques** (in lieu of the *muezzin*, cassette recordings often broadcast the call). Friday afternoons are the official time for worship, and government offices and many businesses close in observance of this custom.

There is a growing religious ardor in Indonesia that can be connected to international developments since the 1980s. Many Indonesians felt that Suharto's corruption and extravagant displays of wealth were contrary to

Indonesian women listen to a speaker at a prayer service outside a mosque. Unlike in some other Muslim countries, women are not segregated from men or forced to veil themselves, although many Indonesian women wear a head covering as a sign of modesty.

the ideals of Islam. In an attempt to gain favor with discontented Muslims, Suharto incorporated aspects of Islam into his personal life. His regime was, nonetheless, both secular and harshly authoritarian. Muslims, as well as Christians, Hindus, and Buddhists, turned to their faiths in a revival of religious identity.

Today, there is a small group of Muslim extremists who support an Islamic caliphate to govern the country and the rest of Muslim Southeast Asia, but they represent only a tiny minority. Most Indonesians continue to support a state that, though it recognizes the major monotheistic religions, offers freedom to worshippers of all faiths. The summary of the 2002 "Islam in Indonesia" conference noted that "there is no likelihood that any legislation would succeed in requiring [Indonesian] Muslims to observe Islamic (*Shariah*) Law. There is no likelihood of Indonesia becoming an Islamic state."

Today Christians live throughout the archipelago. During the 19th century Dutch missionaries were mainly centered in East Nusa Tenggara, the Maluku islands, Irian Jaya, Kalimantan, parts of Sumatra, and Sulawesi. As a result of Portuguese colonization, independent East Timor is almost completely Catholic, as is Flores, where the population was converted by Dutch Catholic priests.

The Islamic and Christian communities have generally coexisted peacefully, though there have been conflicts. One example of such animosity occurred on the tiny eastern island of Ambon, which suffered years of religious violence before a peace accord was reached in 2002. On Java, hundreds of churches were attacked by Muslim extremists during the late 1990s.

Bali is about 95 percent Hindu, and Hindu practice there is influenced by Buddhist and animist influences. Some of the Chinese population has converted to Christianity, though most Chinese practice Buddhism. This is often combined with Confucianism, Taoism, and ancestor worship.

The roof of this traditional Minangkabau home is constructed to resemble the horns of a water buffalo. The predominantly Muslim Minangkabau are one of the more than 300 different ethnic groups that live in Indonesia.

5

The People

Indonesia is the fourth most populous country in the world after China, India, and the United States, with an estimated population of over 238 million people. The population is growing at a rate of 1.5 percent a year, a drop from the annual rate of 1.97 percent during the 1980s. The rate is expected to drop, in part because of a national birth control campaign and family planning program that was encapsulated by the slogan *Dua Anak Cukup* ("two children are enough").

Most Indonesians are of Malay ancestry—they are descendants of people from the Asian mainland who migrated to the archipelago 3,000 to 4,000 years ago. Indonesians of Malay origins generally live in the western islands. On the eastern islands many inhabitants are of Melanesian descent—originally from the islands in the Pacific Ocean northeast of Australia. Melanesians usually have darker skin, rounder eyes, and curlier hair than those of Malay stock; however, many Indonesians exhibit physical characteristics of both groups.

There are over 300 ethnic groups and even more languages and dialects spoken throughout the archipelago. The largest ethnic group is the Javanese, who make up about 45 percent of the population. They reside mostly in Central and Eastern Java, the most populous island. The Sundanese, who live in the uplands of West Java, compose 14 percent of the population. The Madurese, from the island of Madura and the shores of East Java, make up 7.5 percent of the population, as do the coastal Malays on Sumatra. The remaining quarter of the population consists of other ethnic groups and minorities.

On the large island of Sumatra, to the northwest of Java, other major groups include the six strong-spirited Batak tribes in the north who in the past practiced cannibalism and headhunting and many of whom retain animist beliefs; the Minangkabau, a Muslim matrilineal society in the west; and the Atjehnese, a strongly Islamic group in the far north who are darker, taller, and heavier than most other Sumatrans.

The eastern island of Irian Jaya contains numerous ethnic groups, including over 100,000 Dani tribesmen of Melanesian descent who live in the isolated Baliem Valley. They build sophisticated rattan suspension bridges and elaborate irrigation systems. Distinctive groups on other islands include the Bugis, the largest of four ethnic groups on South Sulawesi. Known since ancient times for their seafaring and shipbuilding skills, they were viewed as pirates by Dutch invaders. The Dayaks in Kalimantan are a group of 200 or more tribes, each with its own name, dialect, and customs. They are renowned for their construction of the long-house, a large wooden building between 65 feet (20 m) wide and 600 feet (180 m) long that is elevated on stilts about 10 feet (3 m) high. Built along river banks, the structure can house up to 50 families and may have more than 200 doors.

The People of Indonesia

Population: 238,452,952
Ethnic groups: Javanese 45%, Sundanese 14%, Madurese
    7.5%, coastal Malays 7.5%, other 26%
Age structure:
    0–14 years: 29.4%
    15–64 years: 65.5%
    65 years and over: 5.1%
Population growth rate: 1.49%
Birth rate: 21.11 births/1,000 population
Death rate: 6.26 deaths/1,000 population
Life expectancy at birth:
    total population: 69.26 years
    male: 66.84 years
    female: 71.8 years
Total fertility rate: 2.47 children born/woman
Religions: Muslim 88%, Protestant 5%, Roman Catholic 3%,
    Hindu 2%, Buddhist 1%, other 1% (1998)
Languages: Bahasa Indonesia (official, modified form of
    Malay); English; Dutch; local dialects, the most widely
    spoken of which is Javanese
Literacy: 88.5%

All figures are 2004 estimates unless otherwise noted.
Source: Adapted from CIA World Factbook, 2004.

The Chinese are the largest non-indigenous group. The majority of the
Chinese arrived in Indonesia long before the Dutch. Descendants of this
group generally do not speak Chinese and have intermarried with
Indonesians. The arrivals of more recent years have maintained Chinese
customs, religion, and language. The Chinese make up about 3 percent of
the population and are the richest ethnic group, controlling a large portion

> The Dayak tribes of Kalimantan no longer practice headhunting, but in the past they believed that a skull placed in a basket and cured over a fire would shield the village from harm. The skull was "fed" with offerings of food and cigarettes. Old skulls were thought to lose their magic powers and had to be replaced with new ones.

of the country's private wealth. As a result, there has been a long history of severe anti-Chinese sentiment and repression throughout the country. Most Chinese live in Java and Sumatra, where they are involved in small businesses, banking, and industry.

Over 200 Austronesian languages (a family of languages that extends south from Hawaii to New Zealand and west to Madagascar) and more than 150 Melanesian languages are spoken throughout the archipelago. The national language is Bahasa Indonesia. It is a relatively simple language without tenses or genders and is spoken by most Indonesians in addition to their regional language. Since the beginning of the Suharto regime, Indonesians have made Bahasa Indonesia the primary language of television, print media, schools, and governmental affairs. A common language has promoted a sense of unity throughout the nation.

Education in Indonesia

During colonial times the role of education was to prepare Dutch children and children of the Indonesian elite for government and administrative jobs. By 1940 a system of schools for native Indonesians was established. After independence in 1949, the new government wanted to expand educational opportunities but was hampered by a lack of funds. In 1973 Suharto ordered that part of the nation's oil income was to be used to build new primary schools. As a result, almost 40,000 schools were built or repaired by the late 1980s. But Indonesia's growing population, shortage of qualified teachers, and economic constraints continued to strain the educational system.

In 1975 the state philosophy of Pancasila was incorporated into the curriculum. Today children age six and over study the five principles and learn how to apply them to everyday life. After the third year of school, Bahasa Indonesia becomes the language used in the classroom, replacing the local language. English is the first foreign language that the children study. In general, teachers stress rote memorization and obedience in class.

Some devout Muslims oppose the teaching of Pancasila in schools and send their children to *pesantren*, residential learning centers run by Muslim scholars. At these schools students study the Qur'an and Muslim traditions, laws, and history.

A group of uniformed children walk to school in Kejajar, a village on the Dieng plateau of Java. In Indonesia, children must attend six years of elementary school and three years of secondary school.

In 1990 it became mandatory for all Indonesian children to attend six years of primary school after kindergarten and three years of lower secondary school. By 2004, 92 percent of all primary school-age children were enrolled in school. The same year, 88.5 percent of the total population over 15 could read and write. The male literacy rate was 92.9 percent; the female rate 84.1 percent.

There are more than 50 public universities and numerous private universities in Indonesia. The largest and most renowned are the University of Indonesia in Jakarta and Depok, Gajah Mada University in Yogyakarta, and the Bandung Institute of Technology in Bandung.

Everyday Life and Recreation

Although some elements of western culture have suffused daily life, such as the skyscrapers that dominate the skylines of major cities, Indonesia is considered to be one of the most traditional countries in Southeast Asia. In many villages important decisions are still made by the elders; after the family, the village is the strongest social unit. Children respect authority, and religious and family values are emphasized. The concept of the individual is of minimal importance compared to the family or society as a whole.

Mass media, as well as the Pancasila philosophy, has played a role in unifying this diverse nation. In *Distant Islands*, author Charles Philip Corn, who traveled across Indonesia in the early 1990s, describes the nation's television programming as a mix of censored news, American sitcoms, sports events, various religious ceremonies, and the national anthem sung over scenes of daily life. The programs give the religions an evenly balanced treatment, Corn writes: "If the Christian was called upon to endure a *muezzin* at early evening, he did so with the assurance that a program of Protestant hymns would follow, while Balinese could eschew a Catholic Mass but tune in the **gamelan** dances from the *Ramayana*, the ancient Hindu epic, the next hour."

Young Indonesians often leave their villages seeking employment opportunities and a better life in the cities. As a result, many villages are left with older people while cities have become overpopulated. In Jakarta new arrivals often cannot afford decent housing and live in dilapidated squatter settlements. Throughout the archipelago housing for most Indonesians is substandard. According to a 1995 study, less than half of all houses had a toilet, 24 percent had earth floors, 33 percent did not have electricity for lighting, and 83 percent did not have piped-in drinking water.

Rural tribes, such as the Dani, often live in thatched huts. The Batak live in sturdy multifamily houses constructed with rope and wooden pegs instead of nails. The roofs are higher on the sides than in the middle, and though originally thatched, they are now often built with corrugated iron.

For recreation in cities, families with enough spending money go to the movies, watch television and videos, and visit parks and zoos. They also attend traditional performances of *gamelan* orchestra and **wayang** puppet

According to recent statistics from the Indonesian government, more than 60 percent of the country's population lives in rural villages like this one in Kalimantan.

theater. But for many who do not have these options, main recreations involve family members providing entertainment for each other.

Badminton and soccer are the nation's most popular sports, and Indonesia is a strong contender in world badminton competition. Volleyball is enjoyed in villages across the nation, as is *sepak takraw* (also called *sepak raga*), a Southeast Asian game that combines elements of volleyball and soccer, and is played with a rattan ball.

On Madura, bulls are bred and raced in competitions. Bull racing, along with horse racing and ram head-butting, takes place across the country. *Pencak silat*, an Indonesian martial art, is practiced on West Java and Western Sumatra. Participants fight with their hands and feet, although they sometimes use knives and sticks. In certain areas, especially those with a history of tribal warfare, *pencak silat* contests are performed to celebrate harvests, weddings, and other events. *Caci* whip duels are popular on the island of Flores, and men fight with sticks and shields on Lombok.

Popular celebrations and festivals

Life in Indonesia is highlighted by an array of colorful festivals and celebrations. Diverse ceremonies are held to honor or appease the spirits, gods, and goddesses. Fertility, birth, prosperity, and death are just a few of the subjects on which age-old rituals are based.

The festival of Bersih Desa takes place on Java at the time of the rice harvest. It was originally held to rid the village of evil spirits, but now expresses thanks to Dewi Sri, the rice goddess. During the celebration houses are cleaned and village roads are repaired. In West Sumatra the Tabut festival, held during the Islamic month of Muharram, honors the martyrdom of Muhammad's grandson Hussein and his family at the battle of Karbala. Buraq, a winged horse-like figure with the head of a woman, is the centerpiece of the festival. Buraq is said to have come to earth to take the soul of Hussein to heaven. Townspeople carry decorated replicas of Buraq draped with gold necklaces through music-filled streets, and then toss them into the sea. They then dive into the water to retrieve the remains—especially the gold necklaces.

The Balinese festival of Nyepi celebrates the beginning of the Hindu New Year, which takes place in early spring at the end of the rainy season. Lively celebrations mark the day before the holiday, but on the day of Nyepi all activities stop for 24 hours to trick the evil spirits into believing that the island is uninhabited so they will leave for another year.

On Sumba every February or March the famous Pasola Festival heralds the beginning of the planting season. Horsemen in traditional garb hurl blunt spears at each other in mock battles. It is believed that to appease the spirits and bring a good harvest, some human blood must be spilled, so these battles are often bloody, and sometimes fatal.

Food of Indonesia

Each province has its own style of cooking, but the use of spices and hot peppers is prevalent throughout the country. On Java the cuisine is mild, delicately seasoned, and a bit sweet, but even on this one island there are regional differences. In East Java the food is salty and hot, while Central Java's cuisine is sweet and spicy. In West Java the Sundanese people prepare a crisp, fragrant salad called *karedok* and are skilled at cooking goldfish. The island of Sumatra is known for its spicier food, and beef is used in dishes more commonly than on the other islands. Because pork is forbidden by Islam, it is mainly found in non-Muslim areas such as Bali, or in Chinese restaurants.

Rice is a staple food throughout most of Indonesia, but its preparation varies from region to region. On some eastern islands yams and sago have traditionally been the staples, but rice is becoming more popular as it becomes more available. Coconut milk, as well as coconut oil and meat, are used in many Indonesian recipes.

Indonesian cooks display a selection of savory food at a festival. Ordering the "rice table" is an excellent way to try many different types of Indonesian food at one meal.

Fish is a main source of protein. A variety of seafood is served fresh, salted, dried, or smoked. When *sawah* fields flood, farmers will often raise eels and other fish in the water.

Favorite dishes throughout the country include spicy Indian-style curries; *sate*, or meat served on a stick with peanut sauce; *gado gado*, vegetables served with peanut sauce; *nasi goreng*, fried rice with vegetables; and *mei goreng*, a lightly spiced noodle and vegetable dish. *Rijsttafel*, a Dutch word for "rice table," is an elaborate Indonesian feast that can include up to 40 Javanese and Sumatran dishes accompanied by rice.

Coffee and tea, both of which are grown on Indonesian plantations, are served at meals. Although Indonesia has a predominately Muslim population, alcohol, which is forbidden by Islam, is still widely available.

Textiles and Clothing

Modern textile production can be found in urban areas, though there are still active textile traditions that are 2,000 years old. In many communities women do textile work. In the past, Indonesian traditions maintained that the dyeing of material should be done in complete privacy, and that the women who performed this task should not be sick or pregnant. The tasks symbolized the process of birth and creation, and thus the women were careful not to discuss the subject of death while they were working.

One of the most well-known forms of Indonesian fabric design is batik, derived from the Javanese word meaning "fine point." Flowers, birds, fish, insects, and geometric forms are among the designs used in this distinctive craft. Designers draw on the cloth with a canting, a wooden peg that has a reservoir containing hot wax. Once the drawing is made, the cloth is dipped in a dye bath. The wax resists the dye and is eventually scraped off. The process is repeated until the desired colors or patterns have been achieved. In the 19th century, to compete with inexpensive printed European cloth, a large copper stamp was used to make the patterns, thus increasing speed and production. Batik was traditionally made only by women. Today, both men and women work in batik factories, and the use of synthetic fabrics and non-traditional designs have become part of this thriving industry.

Ikat, which means "to tie or bundle," is the oldest textile art in the archipelago. It is similar to the Western craft of tie-dyeing. First, cotton threads are bound with leaves or tape to resist the dye. After the dye bath, the bindings are removed and the process is repeated until a detailed pattern is created. Finally, the fabric is woven. The motifs in this craft, made mostly by women, include birds, reptiles, and animals. *Ikat* is practiced throughout the archipelago and is especially popular on the islands of Nusa Tenggara.

In the Islamic areas of Aceh and along the coast of Kalimantan, women use the *songket* weaving method, in which they weave silver and gold threads into silk cloth. The same elaborate style is also used in Minangkaban wedding garments and other formal wear.

Anne Richter, author of *Arts and Crafts of Indonesia*, writes about the mystical properties some assign to Indonesian clothing: "Dress communicates ordinary information about ethnic identity, social status and gender, but more importantly it expresses the relationship of the wearer to the supernatural and cosmic forces." Urban dwellers usually wear Western dress, but traditional clothing is still worn throughout the islands, and each region has its own style. Most of the richly colored fabrics are patterned, and because of the tropical climate, dress is generally simple and comfortable.

One basic item of clothing is the *sarong*, a wraparound skirt, often sewn into a tube, worn by men and women formally and informally. It is usually worn with a shirt or T-shirt. The *kain panjang*, also worn by men and women, is made from a long, wide swatch of fabric and is wrapped tightly around the waist and hips. It is secured at the waist with a sash or elastic belt. The *kebaya* is a fitted blouse made of various embroidered garments. Many women wear a *selendang*, a shawl-like piece of cloth that can be tossed over the shoulder, wrapped around the head, or worn across the torso to carry babies or objects such as baskets. When participating in ceremonies, men will wear a *sarong* skirt, batik shirt, and a *songkok*, a black, Muslim cap. For formal occasions men, especially the Javanese, wear the *ikat kepala*, a head cloth that can be shaped into a turban. In the past, the manner in which a man wore his turban indicated his status.

Arts and Crafts

Art is a respected and meaningful part of life in Indonesia, and weavers, textile artists, woodworkers, puppeteers, sculptors, metal workers, and

A Sumatran woodworker carves a scenic panel in his workshop. Arts and crafts are an important part of Indonesian life.

potters can be found throughout the archipelago. On Bali it is said that each person is an artist, no matter what his or her everyday job may be. Throughout the archipelago many young children study dance and music, and by the time they are adults they are often able performers.

Ancient tribal and religious traditions have influenced the arts and crafts of Indonesia. The Javanese or Balinese *kris* is an elaborate double-edged dagger and a fine example of Indonesian metal craft. It is a ceremonial object as well as a weapon, and is still thought to have magic powers.

Through the centuries Indonesian performance art was used as a means to exorcise demons, reap the blessings of one's ancestors, and appease the departed. Today, the Hindus of Bali and Muslims of Java spin epic tales from their religions through puppet and theatrical performances that are enjoyed year-round by all generations. *Wayang* (Javanese for

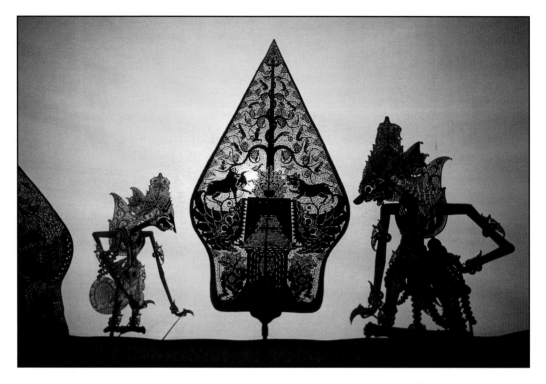

Wayang shadow puppets are the most popular form of Indonesian theatrical art. The puppet shows are often based on ancient stories from Hindu or Islamic traditions.

"shadow") refers to shadow and puppet theater, the most popular form of Indonesian theatrical art, performed mainly on Java and Bali. The *dalang* is the puppeteer, usually male, who manipulates the puppets behind a cotton screen to perform the play. Shadows are made by a light located behind the puppets and the screen. The *dalang*, who studies eight or more years to perfect his craft, speaks the puppets' lines, sings the songs, and conducts the music of the gamelan orchestra to coincide with the play. Traditional *wayang* theater may last from evening to early morning and use up to 100 puppets.

Wayang is often based on ancient Hindu epic poems such as the *Ramayana,* about the adventures of the noble Rama against the evil king of Ceylon, and the *Mahabharata,* about the conflict between the Pandava and the Kaurava clans. Although the conclusion of *wayang* plays almost always is the triumph of good over evil, the stories involve complicated characters and depict complex moral dilemmas.

In Central Java a cycle of Islamic stories about Muhammad's uncle, Amir Hamza, is performed. This hero's virtuous moral and spiritual path is meant to inspire non-Muslims to convert to Islam. Originally, *wayang* puppets were designed to resemble people, but with the arrival of Islam and its rule forbidding the representation of the human form, the puppets were redesigned into fantastically grotesque characters.

The most popular style of *wayang* theater uses two-dimensional *wayang kulit* puppets, made from the hides of young water buffalo. These lace-like, painted *kulit* puppets are used to create shadows on the screen that separates them from the audience. They are manipulated by sticks attached to the puppets' hands and through the center of the figure. In West Java, three-dimensional *wayang golek* puppets, made of local soft-woods, are often used. Similar to marionettes, but manipulated with sticks instead of strings, the puppets perform directly in front of an audience, usually in daytime shows. In *wayang topeng* and *wayang orang*, human dancers wear costumes similar to those of *kulit* puppets and mimic puppet movements to retell epic tales.

The sound of *gamelan* music, which accompanies puppet theater, has been described as "liquid moonlight." In this staple of Indonesian celebration, a *gammel* ("hammer" in Javanese) is used to play many instruments, including different sized brass gongs, xylophones, and bronze kettles. Singing has been part of the gamelan orchestra since the 19th century.

A group of young businessmen wait for a bus in Jakarta, Indonesia's capital and largest city. Jakarta was originally founded in the 16th century; today, it has a population of approximately 9 million.

6

Cities and Communities

*I*ndonesia spans a chain of over 17,000 islands, yet the distribution of its immense population is very uneven. Approximately 59 percent of the country's inhabitants live on the island of Java, which takes up just 7 percent of the nation's total land area. Although there are several large cities in Indonesia, it is mainly a rural country. Except for Jakarta, Surabaya, and Medan, which have thriving metropolitan centers, most other cites are provincial in nature. Residents often live in **kampongs**, neighborhoods where they maintain rural customs. This lifestyle even exists in Jakarta, where the word *kampong* may refer to a cluster of simple buildings, especially if they contain recent immigrants from the same rural area.

Jakarta

Jakarta, the nation's capital, is the largest city in Indonesia with a population of about 9 million. It is located on a flat, low plain on the northwest coast of Java at the mouth of the Liwung River. Prone to flooding, this usually hot, humid, and polluted city has an area of approximately 244 square miles (631 sq km). In 1996 it became a special metropolitan district, acquiring the status and administration similar to that of a province.

Indonesia's capital city is a melting pot of ethnic groups. The Sundanese from West Java and the Javanese are the largest groups. Other groups include the Minangkabau and Bataks from Sumatra, as well as Madurese, Timorese, Balinese, Chinese, and Europeans. The population is mostly Muslim, although there are some Buddhists, Hindus, and Christians. Jakarta has an urban core, but it has been called "a city within a million villages," as diverse *kampongs*, with their own shops, schools, and customs, define the city.

Jakarta is a study in contrasts. It was a boom city from the late 1980s until 1997—skyscrapers, shopping centers, hotels, and a central business district called the Golden Triangle developed during this prosperous period. But just outside this area are some of the country's worst slums. Certain neighborhoods have luxury homes, yet the city is also suffering through a serious housing crisis. More than half of the buildings are poorly constructed and have inadequate sewage and water facilities.

As Indonesia's center of government, politics, media, and business, Jakarta is the country's most expensive place to live. It is a key commercial and transportation hub in Southeast Asia that attracts domestic and foreign investment. Major industries include textiles, clothes, footwear, plastics, metal products, chemicals, and foods. Located close to the Jakarta port is an export processing zone, an area where manufacturers may produce goods for export that are exempt from Indonesian taxes.

Before the Portuguese arrived in 1522, the city, then known as Sunda Kelpa, was a busy port for the Hindu Pajajaran kingdom. In 1527, Sunan Gunungjati, a Muslim leader from the north, expelled the Portuguese and renamed the city Jayakarta, meaning "victorious city." The Dutch and English established ports in the area by the 17th century. In 1619 the Dutch renamed the city Batavia and used it as their capital and a base to send out explorers to discover new trade routes.

By 1740 Batavia enjoyed great commercial success, but was over-crowded with many new arrivals, including Chinese migrants. The government attempted to block Chinese migration and tensions grew between the ethnic groups. In October 1740, approximately 5,000 Chinese were killed by the Batavians after the government ordered a search of Chinese buildings for weapons.

Batavia was considered "the Pearl of the Orient" until European trade ships and increased colonial development brought malaria to the city. By the mid-1700s the thriving seaport became "the Graveyard of the Orient" as the city and its mosquito-infested canals provided ideal breeding grounds for diseases.

Between 1920 and 1940 the city expanded and modernized. The Japanese occupied the capital during World War II and restored the name Jakarta. When the Dutch returned, Indonesian nationalists moved the capital to Yogyakarta, but in 1950 Jakarta was officially declared the capital of the new republic.

Surabaya

Surabaya, the capital of East Java and the second largest city in Indonesia, had a population of almost 3.1 million people in 2004. This industrial city stretches along the Surabaya Strait opposite Madura Island. It is divided by the Mas River, which flows through the center of the city. Surabaya is said to have been founded in the place where a legendary battle between a shark and a crocodile occurred. It is also the site where King Wijaya, founder of the Majapahit Empire, fought Kublai Khan's Chinese army in 1293. One of Indonesia's oldest cities, it has been a trading center and major harbor since the decline of the Majapahit Kingdom in the 14th century.

Surabaya is known as the "City of Heroes" because of its active role in the country's fight for independence at the end of World War II. Today it is the home of an important naval base. The main industries include shipbuilding, heavy equipment, electronics, household furnishings, chemicals, and food processing. Exports from the area include sugar, coffee, rubber, tobacco, spices, vegetable oils, and petroleum.

The city is a mix of Javanese bureaucrats, Chinese merchants, and Arabs. There is an active Chinatown with hundreds of businesses and warehouses. Mesjid Ampel, the most sacred mosque in the city, is located in the Arab quarter. The revered Muslim figure Sunan Ampel was buried at the mosque in 1481. He was one of the *wali songo*—nine holy men who spread Islam throughout Java. Pilgrims come to honor Sunan Ampel by scattering rose petals and chanting at his grave.

Bandung

Bandung, the provincial capital of West Java, is located in the center of the province, on a plateau some 2,400 feet (730 m) above sea level. Founded in 1810 by the Dutch, Bandung is a modern city with wide, tree-lined streets. It was once called the "Paris of Java" for its gardens and parks. Many of the western and colonial-style buildings are now dilapidated, although there are still examples of Dutch colonial and art deco architecture to be found.

Bandung is the third-largest city in Indonesia. The majority of the population, estimated at 2.8 million in 2004, is Sundanese. The arts, dance, theater, and literature of Sundanese culture are studied and preserved

The Jam Gadang (Great Clock), built in 1827, is a popular landmark in the Sumatran city of Bukittinggi.

here. Textiles are a major industry, as well as the production of rubber goods, tea, machinery, and the drug quinine. The city, renowned for its pleasant climate, was host of the Asian-African Conference in 1955, intended as the first gathering of the "non-aligned" countries during the global Cold War.

Medan

Medan, the fourth largest city in Indonesia, is the capital of North Sumatra. This sprawling city, whose name means "battlefield," was founded in 1590 on fertile swampland. At the end of the 16th century and the beginning of the 17th century, it was the scene of battles between the kingdoms of Aceh and Deli. The area consisted of small villages when a planter named Jacob Nienhuys introduced tobacco in 1865. It became a Dutch plantation district after 1870 and a major export center for tobacco, tea, palm products, and rubber. The Dutch made it the capital of North Sumatra in 1886.

Today this large city has a diverse population, recorded at about 2.2 million in 2004, which includes Javanese, Atjehnese, Arabs, Indians, and Chinese. It is considered one of Indonesia's most polluted cities, but it is economically stable and handles a large percentage of the country's exports. The city also supports a large rubber industry.

Palembang

Travel writer Bill Dalton has written that Palembang was "born on pepper, raised on tin, grew rich on oil." Businesses in and around the city account for about 40 percent of Indonesia's exports and Palembang continues to be a major exporter of oil, tin, rubber, and pepper. This predominantly Muslim city, the fifth largest in Indonesia and the second largest in Sumatra, is the capital of South Sumatra. The polluted Musi River, which runs under the enormous Ampera Bridge, divides the city in two parts. Wooden houses on stilts pack the shoreline and floating houses are moored along the riverbanks.

Palembang was the cosmopolitan capital of the Srivijaya Empire from the seventh to the twelfth century. There were 1,000 ships anchored here at one time, and it was not unusual to hear Persian, Arabic, Greek, Cambodian, Siamese, Chinese, and Burmese all spoken in the marketplaces. There is evidence that practitioners of the major Buddhist sect known as Mahayana Buddhism arrived here in the first quarter of the seventh century, about 100 years before Buddhist writings appeared on inscriptions in Central Java.

For 500 years leading up to the 13th century, Palembang was one of the major ports of the world. The city reached its height by the beginning of the 11th century. By the end of the 13th century the Srivijaya Empire had been attacked and had divided into eight smaller kingdoms; by the 18th century Palembang was an Islamic kingdom. Little remains of any of the past civilizations, as many buildings were destroyed in battles with the Dutch.

Oil fields were discovered in the early 1900s and Palembang became South Sumatra's primary location for exports. Today oil refining, cement manufacturing, and fertilizer production are major industries in this city of approximately 1.5 million people.

Yogyakarta

Yogyakarta is 18 miles (29 km) inland from Java's southern coast, near the active volcano Mount Merapi (Fire Mountain). Also known as Yogya, the city is surrounded by Java's ancient ruins and located in the center of the island's "realm of the dead." It has a population of approximately 490,000.

Yogyakarta is known as a longtime symbol of national resistance. The Dutch arrival in the area in 1602 was met with rebellion. In 1755 Prince Mangkubumi, the leader of the most powerful independent Javanese state,

An Indonesian farmer prepares a field for his third rice crop of the year near Yogykarta. This city on the southern coast of Java is home to nearly half a million Indonesians.

built a ***kraton***—a small, walled fortified palace city—and named it Yogyakarta. But Yogyakarta's independence could not last. It was sacked by the British in 1811 and finally came under Dutch rule by 1830.

In 1948 the sultan of Yogyakarta locked himself in his *kraton* and negotiated with the Dutch from the top of his palace, looking down on the colonists with his subjects watching. The Dutch could not act against the popular sultan without creating a riot among the people, who viewed him as a god. As a result, after independence, Yogya was granted special status as a self-governing district, responsible directly to Jakarta. One popular sultan of the city, Hamengkubuwono IX, was Suharto's vice president from 1973 to 1978.

Today Yogyakarta continues to be headed by a sultan in this royal line, Hamengkubuwono X, and the *kraton* is the focus of traditional life. The city is considered the cultural capital of Java—as a center of higher learning, art, music, *wayang* theater, and batik making. It is a popular tourist destination and is known for its hand-tooled silver and leather products. Tanneries, textile mills, and pharmaceutical factories contribute to the region's economy.

About 26 miles (42 km) northwest of Yogyakarta, on top of a small hill, is Borobudhur, the largest Buddhist shrine in the world. Called "one of the most imposing creations of mankind," it was built between A.D. 778 and 850 by the rulers of the Sailendra dynasty. Sir Thomas Raffles, the British governor of Java, had the long-abandoned site cleared of centuries of volcanic ash and growth in 1815. Restoration of the monument resumed in 1973 with the assistance of the United Nations Educational, Scientific and Cultural Organization (UNESCO).

Borobudhur was designed in the form of a giant *stupa*, a bell-shaped burial place. From above it resembles a giant *mandala*, or meditation wheel. The monument, which is composed of over 2 million cubic feet of stone, is thought to represent Buddha's view of the cosmos—grounded in the earthly world and spiraling up to the heavens.

Bali

The densely populated Hindu island of Bali, just over 1 mile (2 km) from the far eastern tip of Java, has been called a "fossilized Java, a living museum of the old Indo-Javanese civilization." Populated since prehistoric times, stone inscriptions date from about ninth century A.D., when the island already had a sophisticated irrigation system for growing rice. From A.D. 1019 Hindu Java began to influence the region. In 1343 Gajah Mada of Java's Majapahit Empire conquered the island and began shaping its religious and cultural life. With the rise of Islam on Java during the 15th century, the empire collapsed and many intellectuals, artists, and leaders migrated to Bali, bringing their Hindu culture and sacred texts.

A Balinese dancer performs in an outdoor theater. Bali's unique culture makes the island very different from the rest of Indonesia.

Because of this Hindu influx, the people of Bali developed unique Hindu customs, which were often joined together with their existing animist beliefs.

When the Dutch arrived in 1597 they thought they had discovered heaven on earth in this magnificent landscape. But the Balinese fiercely resisted the colonists. Even after the Dutch conquered northern Bali in 1846, the resistance continued. In 1906, when the Dutch began a naval bombardment of the town of Denpasar to tighten their control of the region, Balinese royalty, dressed in ceremonial garb, walked directly into Dutch fire in a suicidal march. The royal figures were joined by their followers—almost 4,000 people in total—in a sacred act known as ***puputan***. When the Dutch returned after World War II, a Balinese resistance group again committed *puputan* in the Battle of Marga.

This idyllic island has also suffered recent tragedies: in 1963 thousands were killed when the volcano Gunung Agung erupted; in 1965 Bali experienced some of the worst anti-communist massacres in Indonesia; and in October 2002, a terrorist bomb in a nightclub in Kuta intended for Westerners killed 202 people, including many Indonesian employees.

The tropical beauty and rich culture of Bali have made it a popular tourist destination, and it is now being revitalized after the terrorist attack. The arts, especially wood crafting, dance, gamelan, and sculpture, continue to flourish. The capital, Denpasar, is the largest city on Bali with a population of some 500,000. It has a cosmopolitan atmosphere and hosts one of the largest, busiest markets on the island.

Aceh and Banda Aceh

Aceh (also spelled *Atjeh*), Sumatra's northernmost province, was one of the first centers of Islam in the archipelago. In 1292 Marco Polo visited the sultanate and noted the Islamic presence and the six busy ports. In 1585 the sultan of Aceh sent a letter to Queen Elizabeth I in which he wrote, "I am the mighty ruler of the Regions below the wind, who holds sway over the land of Aceh and over the land of Sumatra and over all the lands tributary to Aceh, which stretch from the sunrise to the sunset." By exalting the potential wealth of the region, this letter initiated a trade agreement between Aceh and England that lasted until the 19th century.

Banda Aceh, the capital, reached its apex of prosperity in the 17th century when it was a commercial, intellectual, and spiritual center. Gold, tortoiseshell, pepper, and camphor were major exports. It began to decline by the end of the century. The region remained free of Dutch rule until 1871. In 1873 the Dutch attacked Aceh, and the ensuing Aceh War lasted over 30 years, until the Dutch achieved a kind of negotiated victory.

During World War II the Japanese experienced a short-lived welcome in the area, and in 1951 the Indonesian government tried to incorporate Aceh's territory into neighboring North Sumatra. The region's militant Muslims, opposed to Jakarta's secular government, declared they did not want to merge with the Christian Bataks of North Sumatra, and in 1953 proclaimed Aceh an independent Islamic republic.

In May 1959, Aceh was granted special provincial status with religious, cultural, and educational autonomy. Islam is observed in Aceh in a more orthodox manner than in other parts of the archipelago. Banda Aceh is known as the "doorway to Mecca," as it has long been a stop for pilgrims traveling to the holy city. In this sprawling metropolis of about 150,000 people, the Atjehnese language is written in Arabic script and almost all businesses close at important prayer times and for Muslim holidays. It is

Atjehnese activitsts wearing traditional clothing and holding rencong, an ancient weapon, demonstrate against Indonesia's imposition of martial law in 2003. Separatists in Aceh have been fighting for independence for more than a quarter-century.

said that Banda Aceh is the only city in the archipelago where one cannot find food during the fasting hours of Ramadan.

For over 25 years there has been a guerrilla war raging on and off between the separatist Free Aceh Movement and government forces. The separatists want political and economic autonomy for their oil- and gas-rich province. In May 2003 the government ended peace talks, sent in 40,000 troops, and declared martial law. Aceh was basically sealed off to foreign journalists, human rights groups, and diplomats. According to observers from the United Nations, there do not appear to be any efforts to resume peace negotiations, although in 2004 the Indonesian government downgraded the security status from martial law to a state of emergency.

Indonesian police escort militant Muslim cleric Abu Bakar Bashir through the hallway of a Jakarta mosque. Bashir is believed to be the head of the radical Muslim group Jemaah Islamiyah, which is responsible for terrorist bombings on Bali and other islands. Indonesia's government has worked with the United States, as well as with its regional neighbors, to fight terrorism by Islamist groups.

7

Foreign Relations

*I*ndonesia's position as the largest country in Southeast Asia and the largest Muslim nation in the world has shaped its foreign relations. Over several centuries, the country has also made full use of its important shipping routes between the East and West.

Under Suharto's New Order government, Indonesia maintained a "free and active" foreign policy. The policy promoted the nation's independent yet committed role in world affairs. Indonesia's goal at the time was to participate in regional and international affairs in a manner that reflected its size and location, while avoiding conflicts among major powers. During Suharto's rule the country took a moderate, pro-Western, and anti-colonialist stance, which has largely been preserved today. The only major policy changes are that the objectives are now less clear and have a more Islamic orientation.

A major facet of Indonesia's foreign policy is its membership in the Association of Southeast Asian Nations (ASEAN). This organization was founded on August 8, 1967, by Indonesia, Malaysia, Singapore, Thailand, and the Philippines to strengthen economic growth, peace, and stability in the region. Today its members also include Brunei, Vietnam, Laos, Myanmar (formerly Burma), and Cambodia. To promote relations with its

Foreign ministers from various Asian countries take part in a 2004 ASEAN meeting in Jakarta. Indonesia was a founding member of this international organization, which was formed to strengthen the nations of Southeast Asia economically and socially.

eastern and southern neighbors, Indonesia is active in the Pacific Islands Forum, the Southwest Pacific Dialogue, and the Tripartite Consultation with Australia and East Timor.

As the largest Muslim nation, Indonesia has been a member of the Organization of the Islamic Conference (OIC) since 1969. Among OIC members Indonesia usually is a moderate voice—a reflection of its multi-religious nature. The country considers Islamic solidarity as it makes decisions of foreign policy. For example, like all Muslim countries, Indonesia officially professes support for the establishment of an independent Palestinian state.

Regional Relations

Neighboring Japan supports Indonesia's reforms and its attempts at economic stability. Japan has a strong economic presence in the country as the largest donor of developmental aid and the recipient of over 50 percent of Indonesia's exports. The relationship between the states has been strengthened by Japan's assistance in developing Indonesia's infrastructure and its police force.

Japan does not support the separatist movement in Aceh, but the country has contributed to the province's emergency assistance fund for orphans, widows, and persons displaced by the conflict. On December 3, 2002, Japan co-chaired a meeting with the World Bank, the United States, and the EU concerning the Aceh conflict, to come up with proposals for the reconstruction of Aceh.

Since Indonesia and China reestablished diplomatic ties in 1990, the two countries have maintained a supportive and positive relationship. Relations were suspended in 1967 after the alleged communist coup in Indonesia, because the Suharto government claimed Beijing was supporting the Indonesian Communist Party (PKI). The renewed ties boosted political and economic relations and led to the renewed citizenship status of approximately 300,000 stateless residents of Chinese descent.

Indonesia's relations with Australia, its neighbor to the south, have often been strained. Tensions heightened in 1986 when the Australian press ran a story that exposed the corruption in President Suharto's family. The incident led to a temporary ban on Australian journalists in Indonesia. Another source of disagreement is over East Timor. Australia had historically recognized Indonesia's claim to East Timor, and in 1989 the two countries signed a treaty to mutually exploit the oil-rich waters between Timor and Australia. In 1991 demonstrations at the Indonesian embassy in Canberra, Australia, protesting Indonesia's East Timor policy led to angry diplomatic exchanges between the two countries that were eventually resolved. However, when Australia took a larger role in peacekeeping efforts in East Timor to end the violence after the 1999 vote for independence, relations again became strained.

Ties between the Indonesian and Australian governments have warmed since the 2002 Bali bombing, in which 88 Australian tourists were among the victims. The attack led to greater police and military cooperation between the two Pacific nations. Australia pledged more than $26 million to build a joint counterterrorism center in Jakarta, and agreed to help train Indonesian counterterrorism forces. The country also promised $7 million to strengthen Indonesian law-enforcement agencies.

Indonesian terrorists took note of Australia's increased support. On September 9, 2004, a member of the Indonesian terrorist group Jemaah Islamiya, which has been linked to al-Qaeda, detonated a car bomb outside the gates of the Australian embassy in Jakarta. Nine Indonesians were killed and more than 180 people injured in the blast. Jemaah Islamiya had previously been responsible for the Bali bombing and an August 2003 attack on the Marriott Hotel in Jakarta.

"There's been extraordinary cooperation between the Australian Federal Police and Indonesian police and wide-ranging cooperation on terrorism," Phillip Flood, a former ambassador to Indonesia, told the

Australian Broadcasting Corporation. "But clearly there has to be much, much more and a more accelerated effort by Indonesia to tackle this [terror] problem at its source."

Relations with the Philippines and Malaysia

The Philippines is an archipelago located just to the northeast of Borneo. It is the only Christian country in Asia; 83 percent of the population is Roman Catholic and 9 percent is Protestant. Muslims, who make up 5 percent, are the largest minority, and mainly reside on the island of Mindanao and in the Sulu archipelago. In February 1986, Ferdinand Marcos was overthrown after leading as the country's dictator for 21 years. According to M. C. Ricklefs, the move toward democracy in the Philippines "was particularly ominous for [Suharto], for there were many parallels and personal links between the two corrupt and oppressive regimes."

Officially, Indonesia welcomed the new president of the Philippines, Corazon Aquino. In August 1986, Aquino made her first foreign visit to Indonesia. During her trip Suharto promised he would not aid the Muslim separatists on Mindanao, but advised Aquino not to tolerate the communist insurgents in her country. Relations between the two countries were stable throughout the 1990s, although Muslim extremists continue to be an issue in the southern Philippine islands close to Indonesia.

Indonesia's relations with Malaysia have improved since Sukarno publicly protested the creation of the new country in 1963. Along with Indonesia, Malaysia was one of the founding members of ASEAN and has made regional stability the cornerstone of its foreign policy. Their relationship has been reinforced by the fact that both countries have large Muslim populations and are similar racially, culturally, and linguistically. Under Suharto, there were problems concerning illegal Indonesian immigrants in Malaysia and Malaysia's exportation of radical Islamic audiotapes into

Indonesia. There have also been border disputes over the two small islands of Sipadan and Ligitan to the north of Borneo. The International Court of Justice acknowledged Malaysia's claim to these islands in 2002.

Relations with Europe and the United States

The European Commission of the European Union (EU) began holding friendly talks with Indonesia in the 1970s. The legal basis for the alliance was established in the 1980 EU-ASEAN Agreement. One of the goals of the European Union is to help Indonesia strengthen its "social safety net" through local charities and assistance in family planning, health, and education. The EU is Indonesia's second-largest trading partner (after Japan), and in 2001 was the largest recipient of Indonesian exports other than oil and gas.

Indonesia's activities in East Timor had a negative effect on European relations, but after the formal recognition of the independent state in May 2002, the EU stated that it could make a new start with Indonesia. Today, the EU supports Indonesia's policy of decentralization, as well as special autonomy legislation for the provinces of Aceh and Papua within the state of Indonesia. In a statement issued on May 19, 2003, the General Affairs and External Relations Council of the EU appealed to Jakarta and Aceh to resume negotiations and fully honor the agreement to end hostilities they signed on December 9, 2002.

Indonesia and the United States enjoy cordial relations and the common goals of promoting peace, stability, and security in Southeast Asia. Although the countries do not share a formal diplomatic or security treaty, the United States supports Indonesia's advances toward democracy, its attempts at decentralization, and its efforts to improve the economy. Cooperation in the war on terrorism is a key factor in the countries' relationship.

The United States supported Indonesian independence in the late 1940s and had generally friendly relations with Suharto's New Order government.

During the Cold War the United States showed its appreciation for the government's strong anti-communist position and assisted in the country's economic recovery. In 1991 U.S. trade with Indonesia surpassed its trade with all of Eastern Europe.

There have always been differences between Indonesia and the United States on various issues. For example, the United States has spoken out against Indonesian human rights abuses, while Indonesia issued a strong

For years the United States has had a friendly relationship with Indonesia, but the ties grew even stronger during the rule of President Suharto (right), shown here meeting with U.S. Secretary of Defense William Cohen in 1998. The U.S. helped Suharto remain in power from 1966 to 1998, despite his harsh repression of dissent and widespread corruption in his administration.

statement against the U.S. invasion of Iraq in March 2003. According to Maria A. Ressa, author of *Seeds of Terror*, after the United States attack on Iraq, "The Pew Global Attitudes Project survey, released in June 2003, showed that public support for the war on terror in most Muslim nations had fallen and measured the fall of public support for America in the world's largest Muslim population, Indonesia. In 2000, 75 percent of Indonesians said they had a favorable opinion of the United States. In 2003, 83 percent have an unfavorable opinion of America."

A year before the terrorist attacks of September 11, 2001, U.S. ambassador Robert S. Gelbard briefly closed the American embassy in Indonesia because of threats of violence, and after the attacks accused the country's security forces of "not moving against militants who threatened to kill Americans." However, a week after the attacks, President Megawati visited President Bush to express the Indonesians' "deep sympathy and support for the Government and the people of the United States of America."

Gelbard's successor as ambassador, Ralph L. Boyce, has also been critical of Indonesia's posture on terrorism, but also remains positive. As he has said several times, "As friends we can disagree on a lot of things." In an interview in *The Jakarta Post* he presented an optimistic picture of the future of U.S.-Indonesian relations and stressed the importance of Indonesia's progress toward democracy.

Indonesia's movement toward democracy and its position as a multireligious, predominantly Muslim republic have made it an important U.S. ally in the "war on terrorism." Islamist terrorists have long operated within the country; the radical group Jemaah Islamiyah, which calls for a Muslim state consisting of Indonesia, Malaysia, and the southern Philippines, operates training camps on remote islands. In 2002, the U.S. government promised about $47 million in aid to help train the Indonesian National Police in counterterrorism measures, and another $4 million in military training.

Although some observers have criticized the government for moving slowly against Jemaah Islamiyah and other terrorist groups, today Indonesia is committed to fighting terrorism. Establishing a strong democracy that is supported by the larger Islamic community is perhaps Indonesia's best hope for containing the growth of radical Muslim groups, which are threatening their own civil society.

From inside a mosque in Kaju, Aceh Province, an Indonesian man surveys the devastation wrought by the tsunami of December 26, 2004. By the time this photo was taken a few weeks later, the death toll in Indonesia had topped 170,000.

The Tsunami Disaster

At approximately 8:15 A.M. on December 26, 2004, a deadly tsunami swept out of the Indian Ocean and slammed into Indonesia, instantly destroying numerous communities on Sumatra. Tsunamis also pounded the coasts of other countries in the Indian Ocean, and deadly waves reached as far as the east coast of Africa.

Overall, the tsunami was one of the deadliest natural disasters in modern history, with a death toll of more than 225,000 worldwide. Thousands of people were killed in India, Sri Lanka, and Thailand, while Malaysia, Bangladesh, and five other countries suffered significant damage. However, as reports were compiled in the aftermath of the tsunami, it soon became apparent that Indonesia had been hit hardest. In Aceh, which received the worst damage, more than 170,000 people were killed and another 500,000 lost their homes.

Why the Disaster Occurred

The tsunamis that devastated Indonesia and other countries in the Indian Ocean were caused by a massive undersea earthquake produced by the sudden, violent shifting of two adjoining tectonic plates off the western coast of Sumatra. (Tectonic plates are large sections of the earth's outer layer, or crust.) Registering 9.0 on the Richter scale, the quake was the strongest in 40 years and momentarily displaced trillions of tons of water, creating a ripple that raced out from the epicenter.

Normally, the wave of a tsunami is barely noticeable in the deep open ocean; it is not until the wave gets to the shallower areas closer to shore that it builds to a damaging height. Experts note that an open-ocean swell just 8 inches (20 cm) high can grow large enough to cause damage when it reaches coastal areas. The December 26 wave reached a height of 13 feet (4 meters) as it traveled across the open ocean at 500 miles (805 km) per hour.

Tsunamis are more common in the Pacific Ocean than in the Indian Ocean. That explains, at least in part, why an elaborate system has been set up to detect tsunamis in the Pacific before they threaten land, but no such system protects the Indian Ocean. As part of the Pacific early warning system, scientists use satellite information, seismic sensors, and undersea wave monitors. In the event of a dangerous tsunami, the system can alert residents of coastal areas to move inland or to seek higher ground before the wave hits.

Unfortunately, despite more than a decade of requests by some Indonesian scientists for a similar network in the Indian Ocean, no early warning system was in place when the December 26 tsunamis struck. But

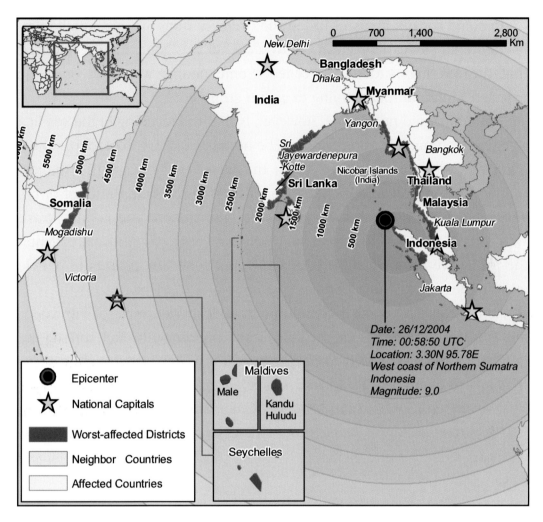

Maldives
Male
Kandu
Huludu

Seychelles

Date: 26/12/2004
Time: 00:58:50 UTC·
Location: 3.30N 95.78E
West coast of Northern Sumatra
Indonesia
Magnitude: 9.0

● Epicenter

☆ National Capitals

■ Worst-affected Districts

□ Neighbor Countries

□ Affected Countries

The epicenter of the magnitude 9.0 earthquake was only 155 miles (250 km) south-southeast of Banda Aceh, and the tsunami struck Sumatra within about 15 minutes. While it is doubtful that an early warning system for tsunamis in the Indian Ocean would have saved many lives on Sumatra, residents of other devastated coastal areas (shown on this map in red) could have been notified to move to higher ground.

even if an early warning system had been operational, there probably would not have been enough time to warn Indonesians about the impending disaster. The earthquake occurred so close to Sumatra that it took the tsunami only about 15 minutes to reach the island.

In some coastal areas of Indonesia, tremors from the earthquake flattened buildings. As people ran out to see what was going on, they noticed that the sea had suddenly receded. Some people went out onto the exposed sand and rocks, trying to gather stranded fish.

What most did not realize, however, is that the receding of the sea is a sign that a tsunami is approaching. The trough, or lowest part, of the wave often reaches land first, and when the water rushes out, the shallow seafloor is exposed. A few minutes after the sea receded, the crest of the enormous wave appeared. Some people who noticed the coming wave were able to flee to high ground; many others were not so fortunate. When the first wave crashed into the beaches, it washed thousands of people away. "The sea was full of bodies," recalled one survivor.

As the wave hit coastal communities, it destroyed most of the wood-and-tin homes, as well as more substantial buildings. In fact, among the only structures that survived intact were sturdy mosques, leading some Muslims to claim that Allah had protected the buildings. Some villages were swamped by more than 10 feet of water, and survivors scrambled for higher ground. Refugees fled without food or water, and some subsisted on coconuts as they made their way to Banda Aceh, which itself was largely flattened by the quake.

The Aftermath

Although the initial destruction wrought by the tsunami was incredible, many experts feared that the death toll might double in the aftermath because of disease spread by the lack of food and clean drinking water, the large number of corpses decomposing in the warm Indonesian climate, and malarial insects breeding in newly formed swamps. "The initial terror associated with the tsunamis and the earthquake itself may be dwarfed by the longer term suffering of the affected communities," explained Dr. David Nabarro, head of crisis operations for the World Health Organization.

To alleviate the suffering, the United Nations sent humanitarian teams to help the survivors in Indonesia and the other tsunami-ravaged countries. The United States, Japan, Australia and other nations pledged millions of dollars to help the relief effort, and U.S. military transport planes and helicopters were dispatched to carry medical teams and emergency supplies to areas where they were needed.

However, the tsunami had washed away roads and airports, making it difficult to move large amounts of food and supplies to remote areas of Indonesia. As a result, in coastal villages like Meulaboh, where more than 10,000 people were killed and thousands of others left homeless, the desperate survivors looted undamaged stores and buildings, stealing whatever food they could find or valuables they could sell for clean water. "People are looting, not because they are evil, but because they are hungry," said Red Cross official Irman Rachmat in Banda Aceh.

In addition to the massive death toll, the tsunami wreaked economic havoc. The coastal fishing industry was shattered by the waves that washed away boats and equipment and destroyed the habitats of crabs, clams, and freshwater fish near the coast. Most businesses and industries were forced to close because of the damage; those that survived the waves were often looted in the chaotic aftermath of the tsunami. Few resources were available to allow business owners to rebuild and reopen quickly. Because salt water had inundated their fields, many farmers in the region also faced the loss of their livelihood; the increased salinity of the soil could make it difficult, if not impossible, to grow crops for several years. According to the Asian Development Bank, the tsunami could impoverish approximately a million Indonesians. "The poverty impact of the tsunami will be enormous," said Ifzal Ali, the bank's chief economist.

The ongoing war between the Indonesian government and Aceh separatists compounded the problems. Immediately after the disaster, members of the Free Aceh Movement offered a cease-fire so that the humanitarian

The scope of the disaster is evident in this aerial photo of Banda Aceh, taken January 16, 2005. Three weeks earlier, this had been a bustling provincial capital of some 150,000 residents; now only a few scattered houses can be seen amid the still-flooded landscape.

crisis could be addressed. The government accepted, but the rebels later said that the government was using the crisis as an opportunity to continue waging its war against dissidents. For its part, the government claimed that rebels had attacked aid convoys. By mid-January, Western governments feared that their aid workers might become the target of terrorist attacks, and the U.N. increased security.

Despite these problems, the relief and cleanup effort was quickly organized. Most hospitals had been destroyed by the tidal wave, so medical teams set up makeshift facilities and ministered to the sick and wounded. Tent shelters were erected to house the homeless, and an orderly system of distributing food and water was established. The areas around refugee camps were sprayed to kill insects that might spread malaria and other communicable diseases. Because most people had lost their livelihoods, relief organizations paid them to clean up rubble, open roads, and collect dead bodies. Workers tried to identify bodies before they were quickly buried in mass graves (to prevent the spread of disease), but that was not always possible. Although the leaders of the relief effort were pleased with the progress, they agreed that the cleanup of communities in Aceh would probably take years.

Many people who lost everything they had in the disaster took solace in their faith. Muslims believe that Allah allows and controls everything that happens, and even natural disasters include signs of His mercy and compassion, explains Akbar Ahmed, chair of Islamic studies at American University. "On the individual level, [Muslims] also have this notion that God is testing them by taking away a child or a spouse," says Ahmed. "Will you lose your faith or will you continue to believe?" This idea of testing provides a "built-in psychological cushion which allows Muslims to absorb a tragedy of this scale," he said.

"I was never very religious before," commented one Indonesian survivor, who had walked nearly 200 miles to reach Banda Aceh after his village was destroyed. "But I find I'm only really at peace these days when I'm in the mosque. There are moments I get angry, though. I ask God: Why, why, why?" Another survivor, a 17-year-old boy who was among the student volunteers cleaning a mosque in Banda Aceh, was perhaps better able to explain the increase in religious fervor. "Everything changed," he said. "We saw the fury of God. We saw it face to face."

ca. 2000–500 B.C.	Various peoples of the Asian mainland gradually migrate southward toward Indonesia.
ca. 100 B.C.	Traditional Indonesian artistic traditions begin to flourish.
A.D. 600–1200s	Srivijaya, the first major Buddhist kingdom, becomes a great sea power and establishes its base in Palembang, Sumatra.
Early 700s	The Hindu Mataram dynasty controls central Java.
750–850	The Buddhist Sailendra dynasty controls central Java.
778–850	The Sailendra dynasty builds Borobudhur.
1292	Marco Polo visits North Sumatra.
1300s	The Hindu-Buddhist Majapahit Kingdom controls much of Indonesia.
1400s	Islam spreads through the archipelago.
1511	The Portuguese capture Malacca.
Late 1500s	Portuguese and Spanish priests introduce Christianity to the eastern islands.
1596	The Dutch arrive in West Java to pursue spice trade.
1602	The Dutch East India Company (VOC) is formed.
1620s	The Dutch take control over parts of the archipelago.
1799	The VOC charter lapses and the Dutch government takes over the VOC's Indonesian territory.
1811–16	The British take temporary control of the Dutch East Indies during the Napoleonic Wars in Europe.
1816	Dutch authority is reestablished in Indonesia.

Chronology

1821–38	In the Padri War, religious and secular leaders fight in the Minangkabau region of North Sumatra.
1825–30	The Dutch put down a guerilla revolt known as the Java War.
1873–1904	In the Aceh War, Muslims and the Dutch fight over the Aceh region, which the Netherlands eventually gains.
1883	The Krakatau volcano erupts in Sunda Strait.
1891	Eugene Dubois discovers homonid remains he names "Java Man."
1911	The nationalist movement Sarekat Islam is organized.
1942–45	Japanese forces occupy Indonesia.
1945	Indonesia proclaims independence from the Dutch on August 17; Sukarno becomes first president of an independent Indonesia.
1949	The Republic of Indonesia is officially established on December 27; the Dutch continue to control Irian Jaya and the Portuguese maintain their hold on East Timor.
1955	Indonesia hosts the Bandung Conference of non-aligned nations; the first parliamentary elections are held.
1959	Sukarno imposes concept of Guided Democracy.
1965	Six generals are assassinated in attempted coup on September 30.
1966	Sukarno signs power over to Suharto.
1967	Indonesia becomes founding member of ASEAN; Suharto is named acting president.
1968	Suharto is officially inaugurated as president.

1969	Irian Jaya is incorporated as Indonesia's 26th province.
1976	East Timor, forcibly annexed, is made Indonesia's 27th province.
1997	The Asian financial crisis hits Indonesia in July.
1998	Four students are killed during a protest at Trisakti University; riots and protests in Jakarta and other cities result in Suharto's resignation on May 21; B. J. Habibie is sworn in as Indonesia's third president.
1999	The vote for East Timor's autonomy results in its independence; Abdurrahman Wahid is elected fourth president of Indonesia.
2001	President Wahid is impeached; the People's Consultative Assembly (MPR) installs Megawati Sukarnoputri as the country's fifth president.
2002	In October, a terrorist attack in a Bali nightclub claims 202 lives.
2003	Peace talks with rebels in the Aceh region end and martial law is declared.
2004	Parliamentary elections are held on April 5; the first direct presidential elections are held in July; retired general Susilo Bambang Yudhoyono wins in the runoff elections in September; a state of emergency replaces martial law in the Aceh region, though the conflict remains heated; on December 26, a tsunami devastates coastal communities in Aceh.
2005	International aid pours in to help rebuild Aceh.

Glossary

adat—traditional law or custom.

animism—the belief that all living, as well as inanimate, objects have souls or spirits.

archipelago—a large chain or group of islands.

autonomy—political independence and self-government.

batik—a process of dyeing fabrics that uses removable wax.

fauna—the animal life of a particular region.

flora—the plant life of a particular region.

gamelan—a traditional Javanese or Balinese form of music.

gross domestic product (GDP)—the total value of goods and services produced in a country in a one-year period.

hajj—a ritual pilgrimage to Mecca required of adult Muslims.

hierarchical—administered by a formally ranked order of leaders.

ikat—a method of dyeing individual threads in a manner similar to tie-dye before weaving them into fabric.

indigenous—native or original to a particular area.

kampong—a village, neighborhood, or crowded residential quarter in a city where migrants preserve traditional village life.

kraton—a small, fortified royal city.

mosque—a Muslim place of worship.

nepotism—favoritism based on family relations.

Pancasila—the state philosophy of Indonesia, which is summed up in five principles: ketuhanan (monotheism), kebangsaan (nationalism), kemanusiaan (humanism), keadilan sosial (social justice), and kerakyatan (representative government).

polygamy—the custom of having more than one spouse at the same time.

pumice—a lightweight volcanic glass that is used for smoothing and polishing.

puputan—an act of ritual suicide by fighting to the death against overwhelming forces.

rattan—a tropical Asian palm that is the source of the material for wickerwork.

sawah—an ancient method of wet rice cultivation, often on terraced fields.

secular—not overtly or specifically religious.

sultan—a traditional name for the ruler of an Islamic state.

syncretistic—referring to the blending of different religions, practices, or philosophies.

wayang—dramatic puppet theater.

Further Reading

Bangs, Richard, and Christian Kallen. *Islands of Fire, Islands of Spice: Exploring the Wild Places of Indonesia.* San Francisco, Calif.: Sierra Club Books, 1988.

Blair, Lawrence, with Lorne Blair. *Ring of Fire: An Indonesian Odyssey.* Rochester, Verm.: Park Street Press, 1991.

Corn, Charles Philip. *Distant Islands: Travels Across Indonesia.* New York: Viking, 1991.

Dalton, Bill. *Indonesia Handbook.* Chico, Calif.: Moon Publications, 1995.

Dermout, Maria. *The Ten Thousand Things,* trans. Hans Koning. New York: New York Review of Books, 2002.

Friend, Theodore. *Indonesian Destinies.* Cambridge, Mass.: Harvard University Press, 2003.

Hillen, Ernest. *The Way of a Boy: A Memoir of Java.* New York: Penguin, 1995.

Kartini, Reden Adjeng. *Letters of a Javanese Princess,* trans. Agnes Louise Symmers. Edited by Hildred Geertz. Lanham, Md.: University Press of America, 1992.

Lewis, Norman. *An Empire of the East: Travels in Indonesia.* New York: Henry Holt, 1993.

Richter, Anne. *Arts and Crafts of Indonesia.* San Francisco: Chronicle Books, 1994.

Tan, Hock Ben. *Indonesian Accents: Architecture, Interior Design, Art.* New York: Visual Reference Publications, 1999.

http://www.seasite.niu.edu/Indonesian

This resource has links to sites covering *wayang*, Indonesian literature, folktales, dance, language, and downloads of gamelan music.

http://www.thejakartapost.com

This page provides daily news reports, articles, and editorials about current events in Indonesia.

http://www.expat.or.id

This site offers a glimpse into daily life in the archipelago, as well as links to cultural, historical, and travel sites.

http://www.usindo.org

The website of the United States-Indonesian Society provides current information about USINDO programs and publications, as well as useful links.

http://www.indochef.com

This introduction to Indonesian cuisine has lots of recipes.

http://nla.gov.au/asian/indo/indsites.html

The National Library of Australia website includes links to many cultural and historic sites related to Indonesia.

Index

Numbers in **bold italic** refer to captions.

Index

Picture Credits

The **FOREIGN POLICY RESEARCH INSTITUTE (FPRI)** served as editorial consultants for the GROWTH AND INFLUENCE OF ISLAM IN THE NATIONS OF ASIA AND CENTRAL ASIA series. FPRI is one of the nation's oldest "think tanks." The Institute's Middle East Program focuses on Gulf security, monitors the Arab-Israeli peace process, and sponsors an annual conference for teachers on the Middle East, plus periodic briefings on key developments in the region.

Among the FPRI's trustees is a former Secretary of State and a former Secretary of the Navy (and among the FPRI's former trustees and interns, two current Undersecretaries of Defense), not to mention two university presidents emeritus, a foundation president, and several active or retired corporate CEOs.

The scholars of FPRI include a former aide to three U.S. Secretaries of State, a Pulitzer Prize–winning historian, a former president of Swarthmore College and a Bancroft Prize–winning historian, and two former staff members of the National Security Council. And the FPRI counts among its extended network of scholars—especially its Inter-University Study Groups—representatives of diverse disciplines, including political science, history, economics, law, management, religion, sociology, and psychology.

DR. HARVEY SICHERMAN is president and director of the Foreign Policy Research Institute in Philadelphia, Pennsylvania. He has extensive experience in writing, research, and analysis of U.S. foreign and national security policy, both in government and out. He served as Special Assistant to Secretary of State Alexander M. Haig Jr. and as a member of the Policy Planning Staff of Secretary of State James A. Baker III. Dr. Sicherman was also a consultant to Secretary of the Navy John F. Lehman Jr. (1982–1987) and Secretary of State George Shultz (1988).

A graduate of the University of Scranton (B.S., History, 1966), Dr. Sicherman earned his Ph.D. at the University of Pennsylvania (Political Science, 1971), where he received a Salvatori Fellowship. He is author or editor of numerous books and articles, including *America the Vulnerable: Our Military Problems and How to Fix Them* (FPRI, 2002) and *Palestinian Autonomy, Self-Government and Peace* (Westview Press, 1993). He edits *Peacefacts*, an FPRI bulletin that monitors the Arab-Israeli peace process.

LYNDA COHEN CASSANOS is a freelance writer and editor. She is the author of *Morocco* (Mason Crest Publishers, 2004) and *Sutter's Fort and the California Gold Rush* (Mason Crest Publishers, forthcoming). A graduate of the University of California, Berkeley, she is an avid traveler with an interest in Southeast Asia and world religions. Lynda Cohen Cassanos lives in Manhattan with her husband and two children.